FINANCIAL SECTOR OF THE AMERICAN ECONOMY

edited by

STUART BRUCHEY
Allan Nevins Professor Emeritus
Columbia University

A GARLAND SERIES

CENTRAL BANK AUTONOMY

THE FEDERAL RESERVE SYSTEM IN AMERICAN POLITICS

J. KEVIN CORDER

GARLAND PUBLISHING, INC.
A MEMBER OF THE TAYLOR & FRANCIS GROUP
NEW YORK & LONDON / 1998

Library of Congress Cataloging-in-Publication Data

Corder, J. Kevin, 1964–
Central bank autonomy : the Federal Reserve System in American politics / J. Kevin Corder.
p. cm. — (Financial sector of the American economy)
Revision of the author's doctoral dissertation
Includes bibliographical references and index.
ISBN 0-8153-3197-5 (alk. paper)
1. Board of Governors of the Federal Reserve System (U.S.) 2. Federal Reserve banks. 3. Monetary policy—United States. I. Title. II. Series.
HG2563.C66 1998
332.1'1'0973—dc21

98-25627

Printed on acid-free, 250-year-life paper
Manufactured in the United States of America

To my mother and the memory of my father

Contents

Tables and Figures

TABLES

FIGURES

Acknowledgments

I am indebted to a number of people for assistance and support in this project. In the early stages of the research I benefited from the help of Barbara Salert and frequent collaboration with Robert Foley and Stephen Lewis. Jack Knight and Andy Sobel undertook the burden of reading and commenting on many of the early drafts. I feel I owe much to John Sprague. His encouragement and enthusiasm for the project helped to convince me that I could complete the research and produce an interesting manuscript. Financial support from the Department of Political Science and the Graduate School of Arts and Sciences at Washington University, the Eisenhower World Affairs Institute, and the Gerald R. Ford Foundation made it possible to for me to visit the presidential libraries and write the book. Many of the consultants in the Social Science Computing Facility at Washington University have influenced my thinking in one way or another and I benefited from working with them. Michael McBurnett, Paul Wahlbeck, Chris Gilbert, Gunther Hega, and Andrew Whitford deserve particular mention. Students in the Foundations of American Politics seminars at Western Michigan University have also compelled me to update my conclusions and refine my claims about the Fed. Finally, I owe a great debt to my wife, Kathy, for her unfailing support, ingenious culinary incentives, and encouraging words.

Abbreviations

ABA	American Bankers Association
CEA	Council of Economic Advisers
DIDMCA	Depository Institutions Deregulation and Monetary Control Act of 1980
Fed	Federal Reserve System
FOMC	Federal Open Market Committee
GAO	General Accounting Office

Central Bank Autonomy

CHAPTER 1

The Puzzle of Central Bank Autonomy

The Federal Reserve System, the nation's central bank, is directed by statute to maintain maximum employment, stable prices, and moderate long-term interest rates. Top decision makers in the Federal Reserve System (the Fed) enjoy long terms of office and have considerable discretion over both policy choices and agency expenditures. This combination of extraordinary discretion and extraordinary control over economic outcomes has generated considerable controversy among observers of American politics and among economists. Some observers of the American political economy lament the formal subordination of representative democracy to the demands of owners of capital (Greider 1987). Conservative economists have persistently complained that political control of the money supply undermines economic stability and performance (Friedman 1962). The development of the contemporary Fed that motivates these criticisms is in many ways an incredible story. As recently as 1949 the Fed was simply an administrative agent for the Department of the Treasury and, as a result, under the strict political control of the president and his cabinet. Thirty years later, the Chairman of the Board of Governors of the Federal Reserve System, Paul Volcker, committed the central bank to a series of monetary policy choices that produced a serious recession. How does a federal agency undergo such a transformation, from subordinate to autonomous, in less than thirty years? Why does the United States' central bank enjoy such a high level of autonomy?

The central claim of this book is that choices by two sets of actors explain central bank autonomy. Key decision makers at the Fed systematically update monetary policy institutions to remove critical elements of monetary policy choices from representative control. Members of Congress tolerate these developments because they benefit from central bank autonomy in two important ways. First, presidents are severely handicapped by central bank autonomy. Second, members of Congress can independently develop new federal credit institutions to protect narrow segments of financial markets from Fed choices. Central bank autonomy is a joint product of the strategic actions of Fed decision makers and the desire of members of Congress to frustrate executive control over monetary policy outcomes.

It is tempting to appeal to formal rules that define the Fed to explain the autonomy of the central bank: the Fed is exempt from the appropriations process and opportunities for appointment of key Fed actors is rare. These formal rules applied to the Fed in the late 1940s, when the Fed was subordinated to the Treasury, and the rules have not changed as the Fed has become more powerful. Remarkably, the statutes that created the contemporary Fed have not been substantially amended since the end of World War II. The structure of the Fed and statutory language describing the instruments of monetary policy are quite similar to language incorporated into the Federal Reserve Act in 1935. This is somewhat surprising given radical changes in the global mobility of capital and structural changes to the American economy that have occurred over time. Absent instructions from Congress, decision makers in the Fed have adopted new technology and new economic expertise to inform monetary policy decisions in an increasingly complex financial and economic environment. Presidents and members of Congress have rarely formally intervened to direct central bankers to adopt particular monetary policy instruments or particular strategies for managing the money supply.

Technological change and economic innovation have compelled decision makers in the Fed to rehabilitate the institutions that structure monetary policy choices. These institutional changes explain the transformation of the Fed from agent of the executive to a remarkably autonomous agency. The institutions of monetary policy are the source of central bank independence. Lombra (1988) labels the several sets of administrative rules and assumptions that are used to implement monetary policy after World War II as distinct "monetary regimes." This label is somewhat misleading, since regime types imply stable sets of rules and patterns of interactions that persist over time. Instead, administrative rules used to implement monetary policy are never fixed for long periods of time. The rules are quite variable. Members of the Board of Governors of the Federal Reserve System routinely update bank regulatory rules, rules defining bank reserves, and rules governing the purchase and sale of government securities by the central bank. These administrative changes have enabled central bankers to redefine monetary policy as capital markets have become more complex and economic innovations have created new challenges for monetary policy. The functions and operating procedure of the central bank have varied enormously despite the persistence of the statutory instructions from Congress.

The scope of the administrative discretion that is given the central bank to implement monetary policy creates unique opportunities for central bankers to behave strategically. Central bank decision makers can use procedural rules to increase central bank autonomy. The technical uncertainty and change that motivates elected officials to grant substantial discretion to central bankers also undermines efforts to exert political control.

INSTITUTIONAL CHANGE AND OPPORTUNITY FOR STRATEGIC ACTION

Decision makers in the Fed have substantial discretion over the types of rules that are used to implement monetary policy. Recent work on institutions and institutional change (particularly Knight 1992 and North 1990) has identified a number of conditions where social actors can benefit from changes in the rules of the game that govern interaction. North (1990) claims that institutional change can have profound impacts on the long-term economic performance of nations. Institutions can affect the relative price of the courses of action that are available to social actors. Long run effects of these changes in relative prices can produce extraordinary divergence in outcomes over time. Knight (1992) claims that social actors may endorse institutional changes that reinforce existing distributions of power, rather than bring about socially optimal outcomes. Strategic motivations may dominate efficiency considerations in a variety of contexts. Since specification of the rules that define the scope and economic impact of monetary policy are left to the discretion of monetary policy decision makers, there is substantial opportunity for strategic action in the process of changing or updating rules. New rules may reflect the strategic choices of central bank decision makers, rather than the unambiguous pursuit of socially optimal control over the supply of money. Over time, institutions that structure monetary policy choices in the central bank may produce outcomes that diverge substantially from the interests of social actors with a stake in central bank performance.

This description of change in central bank institutions is informed by a larger literature on institutions and institutional change that emphasizes gradualism (Ostrom 1995, Knight 1992, North 1990, Thelen and Steinmo 1992). The gradualist perspective on institutional change is quite different than the punctuated equilibrium described by Krasner (1984) and applied to American institutions and outcomes in Skowronek (1982) and Baumgartner and Jones (1991). Punctuated equilibrium implies long periods of institutional stasis followed by short bursts of tremendous change, typically precipitated by internal crises or external shocks. Institutional change is rare, likely to involve conflict, and coincident with visible and important changes in outcomes. Theories of gradual change instead emphasize the persistence and durability of informal institutions (North 1990, Thelen and Steinmo 1992) and the costs of changing formal institutions (Knight 1992). Given the high costs and risks associated with updating statutory institutions of monetary policy, continuous and gradual changes in central bank operating practices are essential for central bank decision makers to respond to unforeseen innovations and shocks. Consistent with the gradualist perspective, informal change in operating procedures, not formal change in statutes, describes the evolution and transformation of the Fed.

Thelen and Steinmo (1992) and Grafstein (1992) emphasize that institutions can be perceived as immutable constraints by some actors at some times and (less often) as objects of contested choice by some actors at some times. Monetary policy institutions that are reflected in the statutory language of the Federal Reserve Act are extremely difficulty to change. These monetary policy institutions, subject to change by elected officials, are ultimately constraints on the behavior of central bankers, on organized groups interested in affecting monetary policy outcomes, and on elected officials. Other monetary policy institutions, subject to change by central bankers, are exclusively constraints on elected officials and other social actors. These rules are only weak constraints on central bank decision makers since administrative authority to update rules is fairly broad. This second set of monetary policy institutions, under the exclusive control of central bankers, is the focus of the book.

WHO GOVERNS UNDER THE NEW (AND CHANGING) RULES?

The policy outcomes produced by the Fed have motivated both economists and political scientists to investigate the relationship between elected officials and Fed policy choices. The study of American monetary policy offers two perspectives on political control of monetary policy. One set of research affirms the subordinate status of the Fed. It has become conventional wisdom among some political economists that the president "gets what he wants" from the Fed (See, for example, Alesina and Sachs 1988). In this context the Fed is best understood as an agent of the executive branch. Monetary policy would be expected to vary as the party identity of the president changes and may be expected to respond to the proximity of elections. Empirical tests of executive influence by Woolley (1988) and Beck (1984) suggest that presidents do in fact influence the behavior of the central bank. Other recent contributions have reinforced the subordinate perspective. Havrilesky (1987) claims that redistributive campaign promises lead elected officials to seek increases in the money supply. Aggressively redistributive Democratic administrations demand large increases; modestly redistributive Republicans demand smaller increases. He concludes that the Fed is ultimately responsive to the demands of elected officials (especially the White House).

A second set of observers of central bank activity conclude that central bank is somewhat autonomous. In some cases this autonomy frees central bankers to pursue policies consistent with social welfare (Rogoff 1985, Alesina and Gatti 1995). In other cases, autonomous central bankers will oversupply inflation in order to enrich their agency (Toma and Toma 1985). From this "bureaucratic autonomy" perspective, political constraints on central bank activity are weak. There is compelling evidence to support the bureaucratic autonomy perspective. First, economists observing legislative activity in the late 1970s concluded that congressional oversight was disorganized and ineffective (Pierce 1978, Roberts 1978). Central bank policy makers exploited technical sophistication and other information asymmetries to foreclose meaningful political oversight. Second, high and persistent inflation in the United States in the 1970s was taken as confirmation of the propensity of the central bank to oversupply money in order to satisfy narrow organizational objectives. Since central bank revenue is directly related to expansion of the money supply, budget-maximizing behavior by Fed decision makers would result in unexpectedly high inflation (Toma and Toma 1986).

An autonomous central bank may be perceived by the various social actors to be a long-run optimal solution to democratic governance of the economy (Rogoff 1985). Recent work (Alesina and Gatti 1995) uses the low inflation experiences of the 1990s to highlight the salutary effects of delegation to conservative (and autonomous) monetary authority. Schaling (1995) and others reveal a direct link between low levels of inflation and formal independence of central bank leaders. In a comprehensive examination of the literature and data on central bank independence, Cukierman (1992) investigates the incentives for monetary expansion and the consequences of central bank independence. It is ultimately the preferences of elected officials (constrained by either high public debt or a large disaggregated financial sector or both) that determine how much independence is conferred on central banks (Cukierman 1992, 450-1). Elected officials confer sufficient independence to optimize the trade-off between potential revenue from inflation and efficient financial market intermediation (potentially disrupted by unanticipated inflation).

THE FAILURE OF CONGRESS: A MENU OF EXPLANATIONS

What about Congress? The two perspectives described above—bureaucratic autonomy and executive dominance—are obviously mutually exclusive. Either the autonomy of the Fed is exaggerated or the influence of the president is exaggerated. The two perspectives do share one assumption: Congress does not matter. Neither perspective can accommodate positive evidence of congressional influence over monetary policy. If Congress influences monetary policy outcomes, then the Fed cannot be described as autonomous and the president cannot engineer partisan or electoral monetary expansions. The conspicuous absence of congressional influence over monetary policy outcomes is necessary for either perspective to be plausible. With few exceptions (Grier 1991), scholarship on the Fed takes the absence of effective congressional supervision of monetary policy as a matter of fact. Why might this be the case? A number of explanations have been offered: the goals and capacity of Congress are limited, central bank preferences are more consistent with administration objectives, or members of Congress have more direct instruments to influence macroeconomic and capital market outcomes.

Goals of Members of Congress and Presidents Differ

The political goals of presidents and members of Congress may be so different that benefits of central bank activity accrue strictly to the executive. Many observers of policymaking in the United States adopt a typology that distinguishes redistributive policy from distributive policy (Ripley and Franklin 1991, Lowi 1964, Spitzer 1983). Distributive policy choices involve the distribution of benefits to narrow groups or geographic areas with costs diffused over large groups of taxpayers or consumers. Redistributive policy choices involve allocation of policy gains and losses across large groups. We expect to observe members of Congress highly engaged in distributive and pork-barrel projects, but relatively disengaged and ineffectual in addressing redistributive policy (Ripley and Franklin 1991). Members of Congress are likely to eschew lawmaking altogether (Fiorina 1989) and likely to devote scarce lawmaking resources to affecting distributive policy outcomes. In this context, broad macroeconomic objectives, especially price stability, have little significance for members of Congress. If we adopt this conventional description of policy objectives and outcomes, then we should not be surprised to observe members of Congress cede control over price stability and monetary policy to the president.

Ability of Each Actor to Influence the Fed

The lack of attention to monetary policy oversight in Congress has been linked to a variety of specific features of monetary policy. Bewildering technical details are at the core of central bank policy deliberations. Legislators have inherited formal constraints on political control of the central bank: exemption from the appropriations process and long terms for political appointees. Roberts (1978) argues that legislators simply lack any effective mechanisms to influence central bank activity. The president enjoys the power to appoint members of the Board of Governors and has discretion in the choice of the Chairman of the Board of Governors (appointed for a four year term). These tools, although limited, offer a control over administrative agencies that is integral to presidential performance (Nathan 1983). Communication of administration objectives is also important. The president enjoys a direct, informal channel of communication with the Chairman of the Board of Governors (Kettl 1986). Formal administration signals to the Fed (mediated by the Wall Street Journal) systematically affect monetary policy outcomes (Harvilesky 1992). The political skills and resources of presidents and members of Congress may be so different that political control of the central bank is relatively easy for presidents.

Central Bankers Prefer Executive Control

If the president dominates monetary policy choices, it would appear that decision makers in the Fed must prefer this arrangement over shared control or direct congressional control. Policy makers in the Fed must believe that congressional apathy or incompetence, each a sufficient condition for exclusive executive influence over monetary policy outcomes, somehow benefits the Fed. Under these conditions we would expect to observe Fed choices that reinforce executive control and rarely observe administration complaints about monetary policy outcomes. Political business cycle theories assumes that presidents determine monetary policy outcomes fairly directly (representative is Alesina, Londregan & Rosenthal 1993). The optimal control variable in these formal models is the inflation rate. The political business cycle describes manipulation of inflation to generate higher than expected economic output in the quarter before elections. The implicit claim is that monetary policy institutions do not constrain executive actions to bring about preferred macroeconomic outcomes. In other contexts, it is argued rather unequivocally that presidential demands are simply accommodated by the Fed. This view is shared by monetarist economists who blame political control of monetary policy for the inflation problems of the 1970s. Representative is Newton (1983):

> The Fed was instructed to participate in the inflationary process initiated by Johnson. The Fed cooperated pliantly with the Johnson demand for increased money supplies, including the provision of a

> sharply accelerated money growth in the 1968 Presidential election (Newton, 1983, 201).

The implication of this perspective is that when the preferences of members of Congress diverge from preferences of the president, the monetary authority will invariably follow the White House.

Scope of Alternatives

Since fiscal policy instruments require congressional deliberation and disposition, presidents are compelled to rely on monetary policy as a flexible tool for macroeconomic management (Kettl 1986, Woolley 1984). Congress has a choice of instruments to affect macroeconomic or credit market outcomes. The president does not. If this is true we would expect presidents to devote substantially more time and resources to influence monetary policy outcomes. Woolley (1984) argues that this type of relationship between the Fed and the president is mutually coercive. The president controls the political resources that guarantee the survival and vitality of the Fed. The Fed controls some of the economic instruments that can preserve an administration. From this perspective, members of Congress are neither constrained by nor particularly relevant to monetary policy choices. Members of Congress can use other agencies and other tools to influence credit market and macroeconomic outcomes. Since there are no strong incentives for members of Congress to affect monetary policy choices, they are relatively weak monitors.

REASSESSING THE IMPACT OF CONGRESS

It seems somewhat incredible to claim that members of Congress do not attend to monetary policy outcomes. Despite the variety of plausible and quite general explanations for congressional inaction, it is difficult to explain unambiguous and controversial long-term changes in American politics—like the growth of the autonomous Fed—without introducing members of Congress. In the period of increasingly independent central bank activity between the end of World War II and the 1981 recession, Congress began to assert more and more control over the activities of other executive agencies and appointees. Aberbach (1990) documents an increasingly sophisticated and watchful committee monitoring system that challenges executive control and intervenes fairly directly in the activities of agencies. Schick (1983) describes a new congressional assertiveness that challenged executive control over substantive outcomes in a variety of policy areas. Finally, observers of oversight activity like McCubbins and Schwartz (1984) have challenged the earlier description of oversight motivations and behavior that informed critical assessments of Congress by Bibby (1968) and Ogul (1976). Our understanding of what motivates Congress and our descriptions of congressional activity have changed in ways that seriously undermine the explanations that have conventionally been invoked to explain the absence of effective congressional control of the Fed.

In addition to the theoretical puzzle, there are compelling historical reasons to believe that legislators monitor and attend to monetary policy outcomes. There have been brief periods where monetary policy issues have prompted extraordinary congressional oversight. Special congressional investigations of the Fed and monetary policy were conducted by Subcommittees of the Joint Committee on the Economic Report in 1950, 1952, and 1966. In the past thirty years a number of members of Congress have advocated statutory changes to bring the Fed under the appropriations process. Other proposed legislation would subject Fed activities to detailed audits, change the composition of the Board of Governors of the Federal Reserve System, and require frequent appearances of the Chairman of the Board of Governors before the Banking Committees of congress. These actions are inconsistent with disinterested legislators.

What are the incentives for this attention to monetary policy? Domestic political aspects of monetary policy outcomes have been described in several works by economists and political scientists (Woolley 1984, Beck 1984, Kettl 1986, Willett 1988, Mayer 1990, Havrilesky 1993, Cukierman 1992). Each of these contributions tells us that elected officials—members of Congress and the president—have preferences over the distribution of credit and over the timing of changes in monetary and credit policy. In much of the work, monetary policy preferences are derived from preferences over ultimate macroeconomic outcomes, especially inflation. The monetary authority has been described as the source of a penultimate temptation for short-sighted politicians: unanticipated inflation produced by the central bank generates short-term benefits for politicians in the form of high employment and relaxed budget constraints (Buchanan and Brennan

1981). Inflation also functions as an implicit tax on holders of money—an alternative to higher explicit taxes. (White 1988, Hetzel 1990, Rogoff 1985). Members of Congress would be unlikely to ignore these tools. Arnold (1990) challenges the distinction between narrow distributive objectives and broad redistributive objectives that is pervasive in the literature on American public policy. He claims that members of Congress share with the president a number of broad macroeconomic objectives. Fiscal policy choices that advance general social objectives (such as tax reform) show how Congress overcomes collective action problems to achieve broader goals. If Arnold is correct, then the absence of effective congressional action to pursue similar goals with monetary policy should be quite surprising. It is not likely that members of Congress would cede control over monetary policy to the executive while challenging executive authority over other redistributive policies, notably taxes.

The absence of overt conflict over monetary policy outcomes is even more puzzling given our experience with divided government. Members of Congress and presidents pursue a variety of objectives in money and capital markets. Members of Congress use tax policy, loan subsidies, and direct loans to encourage a variety of economic activities. These non-monetary credit programs have involved the types of partisan conflicts that we expect to see when economic resources are distributed to particular sectors of the economy. Conflict has accompanied disagreements over the desirability of government intervention in the economy, over the ultimate targets of redistribution, and over the ability of private financial markets to meet social needs. For some reason, partisan conflict has not inflamed monetary policy oversight hearings to the same degree. Divided government has not made it more likely that monetary policy choices are subject to political review and deliberation.

Overall, we are left with an outcome that begs explanation. Why would members of Congress tolerate a federal agency that makes choices inconsistent with the immediate goals of members and, according to some accounts, actually follows the direction of the president?

EXPLAINING CONGRESSIONAL INACTION GIVEN INCENTIVES AND CAPABILITY TO ACT

Contemporary perspectives on Congress and the Fed offer a few possible explanations for congressional inaction on monetary policy. Inaction may be attractive for strategic and informed legislators under a fairly limited set of conditions. First, the Fed may be a useful scapegoat for macroeconomic failures and gains from influence of macroeconomic outcomes may be slim. Second, members of Congress may actually control the outcomes produced by the Fed. Inaction is the observed consequence of effective latent control. As a third explanation, I will make the case below that members of Congress gain a distinct advantage (relative to the president) from central bank autonomy. Each explanation accommodates the occasional exercise of power by Congress and the frequent apparent neglect of monetary policy choices but at the same time introduces members of Congress as informed and attentive decision makers.

Latent Congressional Dominance

Recent developments in the economics of organization have caused political scientists to reexamine the effectiveness of delegation by elected officials. Contemporary scholarship emphasizes the sophistication of members of Congress and the rich strategic interaction between legislators and bureaucrats (McCubbins and Schwartz, 1984). One notable conclusion is that members of Congress realize substantial direct gains from delegation of policy responsibility (Kiewiet and McCubbins 1991). Members of Congress do not simply abdicate oversight obligations when costs of monitoring are large. Agencies are sufficiently constrained by structural features and personnel selected at the "appointment stage" that policy outcomes ultimately conform to the preferences of principals in the legislature and the executive (Calvert, McCubbins & Weingast 1989). Further, potentially uncooperative agencies are highly unlikely to be observed (Banks and Weingast 1992). Overall, we observe congressional dominance of bureaucratic agencies.

From this perspective, institutions imposed by legislative principals constrain bureau decision makers. First period choices about the structure of bureaus, oversight, and legislative supervision determine policy outcomes over an extended period of time. Bureaus, in this context, are simply institutional conduits for the preferences of legislative principals. Strategic choices by bureau decision makers are therefore trivial: structural constraints foreclose strategic institutional change. Alt (1991), for instance, describes the Fed with language sympathetic to this perspective:

> While the Federal Reserve is a nominally independent agency within the government, it is not autonomous. It lacks the ability to set rules of communication and establish the structure of incentives to which others must react—in short, to design the game. Rather, it should be expected at most at act optimally within a set of incentives created by others, its principals (Alt 1991, 43).

It Congress delegates and designs monitoring and incentive schemes effectively, monitoring would not be vigorous and satisfaction with observed outcomes would be high.

The Scapegoat Hypothesis

Kane (1980) suggests that Fed is useful as a scapegoat. Control over economic policy outcomes is tenuous and uncertain. Reconciliation of conflicting demands for price stability and full employment is impossible. Rather than directly addressing economic policy problems that cannot ultimately be resolved, members of Congress and the administration both use the Fed to deflect criticism of economic performance problems. Members of Congress do not attempt to discipline or control the Fed, since the blame avoidance function of the Fed is so useful. Kane (1980) explains the arrangement.

> However good or bad the performance of the economy may be, Fed officials are expected to let Congressmen and Senators blame them for whatever financial or economic developments their constituents back home dislike. In exchange for playing economic policy scapegoat, Fed officials are offered unusually long terms in office and budgetary autonomy (Kane 1980, 209).

Relative Gains

Members of Congress do not have direct influence over monetary policy outcomes. Presidents enjoy a limited appointment power and an extraordinary informal channel of communication to Fed decision makers (Wells 1994). Monetary policy institutions that reduce the informal influence of the executive branch prevent presidents from precisely controlling macroeconomic outcomes. Consistent with challenges to executive hegemony in other policy areas, members of Congress do not demand that the Fed return to the operating practices or procedures that placed monetary policy choices under the strict control of the president and his cabinet before 1950. Members of Congress tolerate and encourage Fed autonomy as a challenge to executive dominance of policy outcomes. Central bank autonomy does not frustrate members of Congress efforts to distribute credit subsidies or redistribute capital.

Evaluating the Alternative Explanations

A generic set of empirical questions are indispensable to an assessment of these competing explanations. How have monetary policy institutions changed over time? What are the sources and consequences of these institutional changes? How do institutions constrain elected officials? Are the rules that structure monetary policy choices more consistent with latent congressional control, blame avoidance, or challenges to the executive? The rest of book explores these questions. My objective is to demonstrate that members of Congress benefit directly from change in institutions of monetary policy that restrict political influence over monetary policy outcomes. I also explore some of the implications of this result. For instance, members of Congress have created a number of federal credit institutions to counteract monetary policy outcomes produced by the autonomous Fed. Small business loan guarantee programs, student loan programs, farm loan subsidies, and federally backed mortgage market intermediaries insulate particular economic sectors from monetary policy choices. Have monetary policy institutions contributed to this proliferation of federal credit programs?

MONETARY POLICY INSTITUTIONS IN THE UNITED STATES

The instruments used by the central bank to implement monetary policy change over time and these institutional changes are typically not challenged by Congress. Technically, statutory rules define the limits of central bank authority to use particular instruments and special authority is often required to add new instruments. In practice, the central bank is rarely compelled to use any particular mix of instruments to implement monetary policy. The Board of Governors of the Federal Reserve System and the Federal Open Market Committee (FOMC) approve very specific rules that stipulate what instruments will be used to conduct monetary policy and to what purpose. Decisions to request statutory authorization for new instruments are rare, but administrative modifications to tailor existing instruments to current needs are common. Action by elected officials, to endorse or to implement new rules, is not required.

The Federal Reserve Act defines the federal structure of the central bank and limits the type and frequency of activities and regulation the bank can undertake. Under the Act a variety of instruments are available to implement monetary policy. Throughout most of the period since 1948 the Fed has relied extensively upon three types of instruments to conduct monetary policy: reserve requirements on bank liabilities, open market operations, and discount window borrowing.

Reserve requirements specify the amount of bank deposits that must be held in reserve to meet the demands of depositors. Statutory limits specify minimum and maximum required reserves. Reserve requirements are fairly stable. Adjustments in reserve requirements typically underscore dramatic policy changes and are rare (less than once a year between 1948 and 1980).

The instrument used most routinely by the Fed is open market activity: the purchase and sale of government securities. The FOMC regularly approves an Open Market Directive that specifies targets, constraints, and objectives of open market trading for the period between Committee meetings.[1] The Open Market Committee consists of the members of the Board of Governors of the Federal Reserve System (7), the President of the Federal Reserve Bank of New York, and a rotating group of four of the eleven remaining Reserve Bank presidents. Under contemporary operating practices, a target for the federal funds rate is established at each meeting of the group. This target federal funds rate is achieved by day-to-day purchase and sale of government securities in the open market. The federal funds rate, the price of overnight interbank loans used by banks to meet reserves positions, influences key interest rates across the market for government securities (most directly the interest rate on three month Treasury bills).

Banks unable to meet reserve requirements in the open market may, as a last resort, borrow funds directly from the Fed. Discount window borrowing rates are set by the Reserve Banks and approved by the Board of Governors. In the early years of the Fed, variation in discount rates across the Reserve Banks affected the geographic distribution of bank reserves and was believed to tailor economic policy to regional needs (Wheelock 1991). Under contemporary operating procedures, Reserve Banks individually petition the Board of Governors for discount rate changes and, when the Board is convinced that a majority of Reserve Banks favor a change in the discount rate, the Board of Governors approves a collective change. Changes in the discount rate typically signal sharp policy changes and are accompanied by a significant "announcement effect." When discount rate changes are announced, other market interest rates move sharply upward or downward as market participants anticipate further Fed tightening or easing.

The practices of the central bank in the United States also include a variety of regulatory, supervisory, and international currency management functions. I limit my investigation of central bank activity to the institutions that affect the conduct of domestic monetary policy. This includes rules that guide the administration of bank reserve requirements, rules that govern Federal Reserve activities in the open market, rules that specify the conditions under which credit is directly controlled, and rules that guide the administration of discount window borrowing. This subset of domestic central banking practices excludes oversight of the payments mechanism and a variety of regulatory roles, such as regulation of the physical security of bank financial institutions.

Research on the Fed by social scientists has yielded few insights into the choice of monetary policy institutions by central banks. Some central banks (like the Fed) use open market transactions to implement monetary policy. Other central banks enforce direct credit ceilings to curb money supply growth (notably, the Bank of France). Why are operating strategies so diverse? Are some instruments more likely to produce political conflict than others?

To demonstrate the effects of variable central banking practices on incentives for oversight and supervision of monetary policy, I document the motivations for and effects of a variety of institutional changes initiated by decision makers in the Fed in the postwar period. I identify the effects of these changes on the opportunities for elected officials to use monetary policy instruments to achieve particular political goals. Chapter 3 examines changes in the structure of reserve requirements and use of the reserve requirement device to distribute the costs of monetary restraint across classes of borrowers. Modification of the reserve requirement can create incentives for oversight by Congress; modifications are therefore very infrequent. Chapter 4 reveals the consequences of Fed decisions about purchases of government securities in the open market. Decision makers in the Fed have considerable discretion over what kinds of securities can be purchased. These purchasing decisions directly affect the monetary policy options considered by elected officials in the White House and Congress. Chapter 5 examines the selective control of credit and the regulation of the end use of credit. Some selective controls, such as direct controls on consumer installment credit, were eliminated immediately after World War II. Other selective controls persisted, notably margin requirements for the purchase of equities. Most of the wartime direct controls have been replaced by *covert* controls such as supervisory suasion or discount window lending restrictions.

In each case, decision makers within the Fed adopt instruments that minimize political conflict over central bank activity. Indirect instruments are chosen over obvious and direct controls. Overt redistributive choices are avoided. Any instrument that abets the political allocation of capital across classes of borrowers is opposed. It is clear that the choice of instruments for central bank activity is not strictly determined by monetary, credit, or macroeconomic conditions. By varying the set of instruments used to implement monetary policy, policy makers in the central bank can exercise some control over the scope and type of political influence exerted by members of Congress and the president. The choices of instruments determines the types of functions that will be undertaken by the central bank. Central bank decision makers must therefore decide if and how particular political objectives of elected officials will be fulfilled before selecting a battery of instruments. Libby (1987) argues that important postwar instrument choices by decision makers at the Fed were preceded by pressures from both System actors and elected officials in the White House or Congress. She concluded that the incumbent president was the decisive actor in conflicts over instruments and activities. I will instead show how instrument choice after World War II creates substantial autonomy for the Fed. The executive is ultimately disadvantaged by this autonomy.

ORGANIZATION OF THE REMAINING CHAPTERS

Three lines of inquiry motivate the rest the book. First, who governs monetary policy? Second, more generally, what can the case of the Fed contribute to our understanding of Congress and the oversight function? Third, how do institutions matter? A number of substantive questions are relevant: What motivates central bankers? To what extent do the institutions of the central bank constrain or frustrate political actors in Congress and the White House? How do elected officials escape central bank constraints to address the demands of constituents?

I investigate the consequences of institutional change in the Fed in three steps. First, in the second chapter, I provide some empirical foundation for central bank autonomy as a goal of central bank decision makers. I demonstrate how policy makers at the Fed behave in ways consistent with the maintenance of central bank autonomy even if this behavior reduces System output, budgets, and prestige. Despite much interest in the political economy of monetary policy, systematic treatments of the preferences of central bankers and the strategic tools at their disposal have been sparse. Many scholars studying the Fed adopt conventional budget maximization approaches to explain decisions by policy makers in the Fed (representative is Goff and Tollison 1991). Pioneering an alternative approach, Chant and Acheson (1972) demonstrated that the of choice of policy instruments by the Bank of Canada is clearly motivated by a desire for autonomy. I extend and provide empirical support for the motivations described by Chant and Acheson. The content of staff deliberations in a series of procedural controversies that required central bank action in the 1970s does not support budget maximization hypotheses. The data support an alternative explanation that subordinates resources or power to the preservation of central bank autonomy.

The second part of the book (Chapters 3, 4, and 5) reveals the effects of specific changes in central banking practices in three areas: the administration of reserve requirements, the use the discount window and selective credit controls, and open market transactions in the market for government securities. Each of the chapters relies on two types of data. First, I identify important institutional changes and the effects of these changes using documents from the library collections of four presidents—Harry S Truman, Dwight Eisenhower, Lyndon Johnson and Gerald Ford. The Truman and Eisenhower collections contain information on the period of extraordinary institutional change following World War II. The Johnson collection contains information on the liberalization of central bank activity that coincided with the end of the term of William Martin as Chairman of the Board of Governors of the Federal Reserve System in 1969. The Ford Library contains information on the changes in operating procedure (and extensive interactions with Congress) during the tenure of Arthur Burns. The Gerald R. Ford Library houses not only the White House documents, but also the papers of Arthur Burns, Chairman of the Board of Governors of the Federal Reserve System from 1969 until 1978. In addition to the library collections, I rely on the annual Economic Report of the President for information on the coordination of monetary policy with other administration objectives.

The second primary source of data are publications of the Federal Reserve System: the monthly Federal Reserve Bulletin and the Annual Report of the Board of Governors. These documents describe and summarize the objectives and outcomes of System activity. The Annual Reports and the monthly Bulletin contain minutes of the FOMC meetings and descriptions of changes in the regulations created and updated by the Board of Governors of the Federal Reserve System. The regulations describe the operating procedures for every central bank activity—from administration of reserve requirements to the regulation of bank lending practices. The Bulletins also report specific regulatory decisions made by the Board of Governors, changes in the key interest rates influenced by the Fed, and innovations in economic methods and expertise that inform monetary policy choices. The Annual Report provides detailed financial statements for each of the Reserve Banks and the Federal Reserve System. Information about Board expenditures and purchases of government securities by the Reserve Banks is contained in the annual financial statements.

In the final section of the book, I investigate the implications of institutional changes at the central bank. I revisit the incentives that exist for elected officials to influence macroeconomic outcomes and capital market flows. I then identify the mechanisms that elected officials used to influence economic activity throughout the period following World War II. The final chapters also outline the implications of this institutional perspective on the Fed for the variety of models of central bank behavior that inform models of the political economy more generally. For instance, monetarist critics of monetary policy choices in the 1970s argue that bureaucratic incentives induced Fed decision makers to oversupply inflation to short-sighted elected officials. Did the procedural choices made after World War II make this oversupply more or less likely? Political business cycle theories presume central bank performance of White House demands. How have procedural choices abetted or frustrated these demands?

CONCLUSION AND SUMMARY

Central bank practices determine the scope of opportunities for political influence of the money supply and credit market outcomes by legislative actors and the executive. Policy makers within the Fed therefore play an important role in the struggle for political control of monetary policy. The mechanisms used to constrain interested elected officials are changes in the rules used to implement monetary policy. The constraints are tolerated by members of Congress for several reasons. First, members of Congress benefit from the macroeconomic outcome (price stability) that monetary policy institutions produce. Second, monetary policy institutions frustrate White House efforts to either manipulate economic outcomes before presidential elections or implement a distinctly partisan monetary policy. Finally, monetary policy institutions do not constrain members of Congress interested in directing capital to particular sectors of the economy. Federal credit institutions proliferate as central bank independence grows over time. The profitable course for members of Congress interested in protecting particular economic sectors is the creation of specific programs that protect very particular groups, not the rehabilitation of the Fed.

NOTES

1. Prior to 1955, the Open Market Committee met infrequently to give pro forma approval to the Directives and policies of the Executive Committee of the Open Market Committee. William Martin abolished the Executive Committee in 1955, it is argued, to broaden the decision making process and reduce the authority and power of the Federal Reserve Bank of New York relative to both Washington and the other Reserve Banks (Libby 1987).

CHAPTER 2

Central Bank Autonomy and the Preferences of Central Bankers

Before turning to the institutional choices that may expand the autonomy of central bankers, there is an empirical question that needs to be answered. Do decision makers within the Fed value autonomy? The question at first seems transparent. Of course, any agency decision maker desires to be free from the constraints of elected officials or at least to enjoy a monopoly jurisdiction over a particular policy area. But this type of autonomy has never been incorporated as an explicit behavioral motivation for central bankers in explanations of monetary policy choices within the Fed. Most analysis of monetary policy choices assumes that central bank decision makers are motivated by bureaucratic imperialism or aversion to inflation, or assumes that central bankers simply follow the changing demands of elected officials. Toma and Toma (1986) and others claim that Fed decision makers, like other bureaucrats, attempt to maximize the resources and budget of the central bank. Alesina and Gatti (1995) and others argue that elected officials, interested in committing to a low inflation macroeconomic policy, appoint central bankers that are inflation-averse. Selection of particular types of central bank decision makers guarantees that a time invariant substantive policy preference motivates central bank policy choices. Woolley (1985) and Alt (1991) argue that behavioral motivations of senior policy makers at the Fed are subordinated to the demands of the White House or the Congress or both.

Although the budget-maximizing central bankers described by Toma and Toma or the inflation-averse central bankers described by

Alesina and Gatti may behave autonomously, they would never be motivated to seek autonomy if more autonomy could threaten either budgets or price stability. Most existing work on central bank behavior simply does not emphasize autonomy as a primary goal of monetary policy decision makers. Political scientists observing social actors in many other contexts—particularly the legislature—conclude that strategic actors routinely use rules under their control to generate autonomy. Institutional change, motivated by the desire to be autonomous, is pervasive (Parker 1992). It would be surprising if managers of public sector agencies like the Fed did not take similar strategic action. In fact, theories of public sector management and change predict this type of behavior. Wilson (1989) discusses the variety of conditions that may lead agency executives to reject higher operating budgets in order to maximize political support. The tactic may be to reduce potential conflict with rival agencies or to keep bureau functions simple. In any case, autonomy-enhancing behavior is commonplace.

There is an important exception to the neglect of central bank autonomy in the study of monetary policy and central banking. Chant and Acheson (1972) argue that incentives related to autonomy can explain important choices of central bankers. Chant and Acheson are puzzled by the persistence of a battery of monetary policy instruments in Canada despite a consensus that open market operations alone are sufficient to accomplish central bank goals. They conclude that a diverse set of monetary policy instruments contributes to central bank autonomy. Chant and Acheson ultimately conclude that central bank acceptance of alternative "institutional arrangements in formulating monetary policy" is contingent on the consequences of proposed changes for central bank autonomy (Chant and Acheson 1972, 15). The implicit critique leveled by Chant and Acheson is that financial market efficiency is undermined by the autonomy-enhancing behavior of central bank decision makers. This behavior would also frustrate precise political control of monetary policy outcomes.

To investigate the extent to which central bankers in the United States value autonomy, I review available evidence supporting the alternative motivations of central bankers: budget maximization and response to political control by either delegation or direction. Central bank behavior offers very little to confirm expectations of budget-maximization or strict fidelity to political demands but does indicate extraordinary concern with the preservation of autonomy. During the

1970s, efforts to preserve autonomy persist even in periods where price stability is unambiguously compromised by central bank policy choices. Autonomy is a persistent goal. Neither price stability nor budget maximization dominates autonomy.

BUDGET-MAXIMIZING BEHAVIOR IN THE CENTRAL BANK

Economists have applied neoclassical economic assumptions to the decisions of bureaus, modeling bureaucrats as rational individual utility maximizers rather than automatons carrying out the instructions of elected principals. Early work on this type of bureaucratic motivation identified a variety of goals and ambitions that could explain the decisions of bureaucrats: organizational loyalties, material incentives, or the personal prestige of individual bureaucrats (Downs 1967). Important contributions to the study of bureaus by Niskanen (1971) and Migue and Belanger (1974) suggested specific empirical consequences of narrowly self-interested bureaucratic behavior. Niskanen (1971) argued that the budget of a government bureau could be an accurate proxy for many of the components of the utility function of the representative bureaucrat (status, income, self-worth). Expanding budgets indicate the successful pursuit of prestige, power, and survival. Successful bureaucrats continually expand bureau functions and budgets. Migue and Belanger (1974) claim that managers of bureaus value the discretion to expend bureau resources on a variety of activities including output, staff, salary, perquisites of office, and activities that increase the chance of agency survival. Migue and Belanger, like other proponents of narrowly self-interested descriptions of bureau behavior, assume that bureau sponsors have a distinct informational disadvantage relative to bureau decision makers. They note that bureaucrats can "raise their discretionary power by overemphasizing the multiplicity of the goals of their organization and the complexity of the production function." (Migue and Belanger 1974, 32).[1]

Strategic alternatives available to bureau decision makers in this context are relatively limited, typically involving manipulation of information. This type of strategic interaction between bureau sponsors and bureau decision makers may take place within the appropriations process or span both appropriations and ex post monitoring. The budget-maximizing bureaucrat described by Niskanen and others (notably Bendor, Taylor & Van Gaalen, 1985) uses program budgets and authorizations as part of a broader effort to signal bureau competence and intentions. Depending on the sophistication of legislative monitoring, it may be in the interest of agency managers to deceive legislators about either the level of effort expended or the level of resources required to produce policy outcomes demanded by the legislature. The strategic neoclassical bureaucrat protects and exploits informational asymmetries to frustrate attempts at political control. In most of the empirical work in this tradition, effective bureaucrats are simply expected to maximize agency budgets under these conditions.

Canonical Budget Maximization Incentives in the Fed

Following the budget-maximization approach identified with Niskanen, scholars examining Fed activity have assumed that System budgets and operating expenses are a good indicator of internal bureaucratic motivations. Some critics of Federal Reserve policies (representative is Toma 1982) use bureaucratic budget maximization approaches to explain what they believe were monetary policy failures in the 1970s. These critics claim that rent-seeking by Fed decision makers explains the oversupply of money in the United States. Since Fed revenue is tied to nominal interest income from Reserve Bank securities holdings, critics claim that Fed managers benefit from inflation of the money supply. The Fed adds excess money to financial markets through the exchange of money for Treasury securities in open market operations. This revenue incentive is invoked to explain the chronic inflation problems of the late 1970s. Revenue, expenses, and employment within the Fed reflect the imperial bureaucratic ambitions of Fed decision makers, rather than the requirements of commercial bank supervision or regulation of the money supply (Shugart and Tollison 1983, Toma and Toma 1986, Goff and Tollison 1991). The notable consequences of this behavior are general inflation (suffered by wealth holders and consumers) and exorbitant revenues from the Fed portfolio, subsequently expended on Fed staff and perquisites.

The financing mechanisms of the Fed create a distinctive set of incentives for central bankers interested in maximizing revenue. The regional Federal Reserve Banks maintain a portfolio of United States Government securities valued at over $350 billion dollars.[2] The interest on these securities is used to fund System expenses and the remainder (now well over 90% of total revenue) is returned to the Treasury as a rebate. The Fed began voluntary rebates of earnings from its portfolio of government securities after the Treasury raised concerns about increasing debt financing costs in 1947 (Toma and Toma 1986). The Fed portfolio and interest income has nevertheless grown substantially over time, with the aggregate value of the portfolio first exceeding $100 billion in the mid 1970s. Fed holdings accounted for 10 percent of the total public debt as recently as 1985. This has led members of Congress to suggest on several occasions that Federal Reserve Bank holdings of securities should be used to retire a part of the national debt. Wright Patman (Democrat, Texas) was the most persistent and vocal supporter of debt retirement. Absent earnings from the System portfolio the Fed would, of course, be dependent upon the Congress for appropriations. This unique financing arrangement creates unique incentives for Fed decision makers.

Does a Revenue Incentive Explain Monetary Policy Choices?

If a revenue imperative drives System decisions and policy, what types of monetary policies should we observe? System income comes primarily from interest on the portfolio of government securities held by the Federal Reserve Banks. The Reserve Banks exchange cash reserves deposited by commercial banks for interest-bearing Treasury securities. This source of income could, of course, be increased by manipulating a few key instruments of monetary policy. Revenue maximizing behavior could be reflected in (1) high reserve requirements that increase central bank cash assets, (2) massive purchases of government securities to convert cash assets to revenue-generating securities, or (3) spending all interest revenue on System staff, facilities, or operations. None of the expected behavior is observed.

Reserve Requirements and System Income

Until 1980, membership in the Fed was voluntary for commercial banks. Members withdrew from the Fed with alarming frequency during the 1970s. These departures eroded the reserves base that decision makers considered essential for the transmission of monetary policy. The use of unreasonably high reserve requirements, for the purpose of increasing System revenue, would have worsened an already acute attrition problem.[3] Until statutory changes under the Depository Institutions Deregulation and Monetary Control Act of 1980 (DIDMCA), voluntary membership effectively precluded the use of the reserve requirement instrument to maximize System revenue.

Open Market Activity and Revenue Maximization

The vast majority of Fed employees and expenditures are overseen by the various regional Federal Reserve Banks. Expenditures by the Board of Governors, in fact, rarely exceed 10 percent of total System expenses. If resources are desired by the Reserve Banks, then Reserve Bank presidents would be expected to support easy money policies (exchange of cash reserves for Treasury securities in the open market) in order to increase System revenue. Analysis of FOMC dissents by Puckett (1984) finds that Reserve Bank presidents consistently dissent on side of tighter money in FOMC deliberations. These dissents threaten the stream of resources from open market operations which are so supposedly so valuable to Fed decision makers (Banaian, Laney, McArthur & Willett, 1988). Key decision makers in the System do not exhibit budget-maximizing behavior.

Federal Reserve Expenses and Federal Reserve Income

The percentage of Fed interest income expended on operations has never risen above 10 percent of total interest earnings since 1965. If one-time rebates are included in the total interest rebated to the Treasury, the Fed has on two occasions rebated to the Treasury amounts exceeding annual earnings (See Figure 1).

There is absolutely no need to increase the money supply through open market purchases of securities or to increase reserve requirements in order to increase Fed revenue. If budget maximization were the primary goal of Fed decision makers, then rebated income would simply be lowered to meet what could be much larger expenditures. Instead, rebates to the Treasury have increased over time. Budget maximization incentives utterly fail to explain the choices of key actors in the Fed.

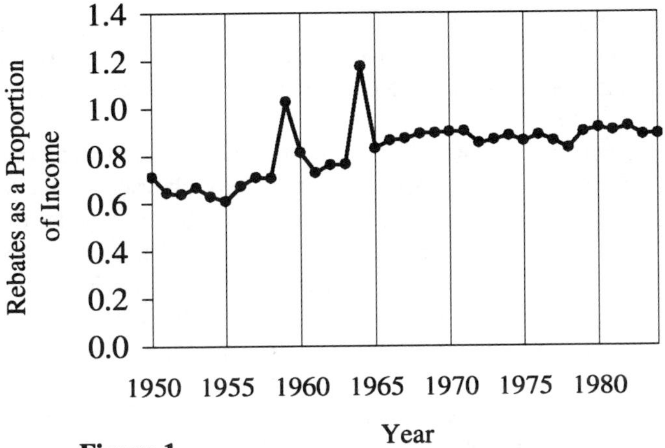

Figure 1
Interest on Federal Reserve Notes rebated to U.S. Treasury, as a proportion of current Fed income (1950-1985).

Source: Annual Report of the Board of Governors of the Federal Reserve System for 1985.

EXTERNAL DEMANDS FOR PRICE STABILITY, INFLATION OR CAPITAL ALLOCATION

Contemporary monetary policy research tends to reject neoclassical bureaucratic models and explains variation in monetary policy outputs as a product of the political demands placed upon the central bank. Ultimate macroeconomic outcomes are explained by examining the demands for specific outcomes (such as inflation) by political actors instead of the demand for outcomes within the bureau. Woolley (1985) argues that the persistent inflation of the 1970s reflected persistent political demands for inflation from elected officials. Alesina and Gatti (1995) claim that the price stability observed in the 1990s is a result of a deliberate segregation of monetary policy choices from political demands: the central bank is a type of commitment device engineered by politicians to control demands for inflation. Political demands could also be reflected in more narrow demands for capital to flow to particular sectors of the economy: the market for mortgages, small business enterprise, or farmers. Goodman (1992) describes how this type of qualitative allocation of capital is implemented through the central bank in France.

These political explanations of monetary policy outcomes, although offering radically different predictions of price levels over time, imply that there are incentives for central bankers to resist political control. External demands upon the central bank may be both variable (alternately desiring and resisting inflation) and inconsistent (demanding more capital for some sectors of the economy while preferring restrained growth of the money supply). Central bankers may elect to resist some political demands and submit to others. Unlike the budget maximizing bureaucrat, it is difficult to make categorical predictions of agency manager behavior under political control without appealing to a more well-developed set of goals that can be attributed to agency decision makers (and that perhaps diverge from the goals of political principals).

With the exception of the conservative inflation-averse central bank appointee described by Rogoff (1985) or Alesina and Gatti, central bank autonomy-enhancing behavior is equivalent to the repudiation of representative control. In the case of the inflation-averse appointee, autonomy-enhancing behavior could simply be consistent with efforts to restore price stability in the face of overt demands for easy money. If central bankers are subject to varied and persistent political demands, then efforts by Fed policy makers to increase bank autonomy are tantamount to efforts to escape political demands. As central bankers attempt to increase autonomy, the transmission of political demands becomes more difficult and imprecise.

Recent debates over the efficacy of Congressional control of policy outcomes have revealed the difficulty in determining precisely to what extent political demands are accommodated by bureaus (Wilson 1989). The congressional dominance perspective described in Chapter 1 predicts a high degree of bureau responsiveness to changes in the preferences of elected officials. The most important variable predicting changes in agency policy choice is change in the composition of relevant oversight committees (Calvert, Moran & Weingast 1987). The preference of members of Congress dominate preferences of other political actors. The signal claim of this literature is that if members of Congress are sophisticated and well informed, we would expect to observe congressional dominance of bureaucratic agencies. These types of explanations typically assume that bureau procedure does not function as a constraint on elected officials and that procedures do not change over time. In short, agency institutions have little effect on the real content of public policy. Some political explanations of monetary policy choices in the United States borrow from this framework (representative is Alt (1991)).

Several critical treatments of the congressional dominance perspective have raised several theoretical and empirical objections to claims of extraordinary congressional control (Woolley 1993, Wilson 1989, Moe 1987). Two of the more serious objections are the lack of precise mechanisms of control available to members of Congress and the insufficient attention given to the institutional details of agency practice (or the link between procedure and outcomes). Extensive agency discretion (tantamount to autonomy) is implied by the blunt control mechanisms available to members of Congress. Formal tools used to influence agency behavior after the appointment stage are costly for individual members of Congress to manipulate. Agency-specific legislation is relatively rare and can offer only blunt and imprecise control over bureaucratic behavior. Appropriations are embedded in a lengthy sequential decision-making process that contains conflicting signals from a number of potentially interested actors. Bureau discretion can therefore be quite broad. Woolley (1993) also notes that the existence of a bicameral legislature creates opportunities for bureaucrats to exploit conflicting directions from interested legislators.

The empirical work that supports congressional dominance focuses on Congress and committees, rather than agencies and agency structure (Moe 1987). Institutional details at the level of the agency are relatively unimportant. An agency could substantially update administrative procedures over time, yet proponents of extreme versions of the congressional dominance perspective would predict no substantive policy change absent changes in the composition of the relevant oversight committee. This insufficient attention to changes in agency procedure causes observers to overlook potential challenges to either monitoring or influence by members of Congress. In the study of regulatory policy and service delivery, a number of attempts have been made to integrate external demands for agency performance with internal constraints and obstacles to hierarchical control (Wilson 1989,

Meier 1985, Wilson 1980). These agency-centered explanations of policy outputs challenge the conclusions offered by the formal models of representative control that inform most scholarship on the politics of monetary policy. Explanations that focus on the behavior of actors within agencies emphasize the constraints and incentives created by agency operating procedure or organizational culture, rather than the institutions or incentives designed by elected officials (Wilson 1989).

Central banking practice in the United States appears to confirm the findings of the agency-centered approach and challenge models of hierarchical control that emphasize congressional design and dominance. Procedural choices have distinct effects on monetary policy outcomes. Opportunities for hierarchical control are limited by agency choices about operating procedure and rules. Central bankers intend to maintain and enhance central bank autonomy through strategic updates to rules, operating procedure, and the structure of interactions with Congress and the White House.

ENHANCING CENTRAL BANK AUTONOMY

Two sets of central bank choices demonstrate the extent to which decision makers in the Fed actively promote central bank autonomy. First, Reserve Bank presidents and members of the Board of Governors resisted the extension of Fed bank regulatory authority to nonmembers in the 1970s. Regulatory responsibilities were perceived as potentially disruptive to central bank independence. Second, efforts by Congress to reassert control over Fed finance and expenditure met challenges from Fed decision makers. Congressional intervention was perceived as a channel for narrow group interests to affect monetary policy deliberations. Reserve Bank presidents and members of the Board of Governors object to formal congressional supervision specifically because particular demands for the allocation of capital are likely to be made by members of Congress.

Case 1: Bank Supervisory Authority

Bank Supervision and Monetary Policy

Complaints about the distribution of bank supervisory authority and the performance of bank supervisory agencies began to draw attention from the White House and Congress in the early 1960s. There was substantial concern that regulatory responsibility shared across a number of agencies at the state and federal level undermined effective regulation and provided opportunities for banks to circumvent strict regulation. The Committee on Financial Institutions (sponsored by the Kennedy Administration) recommended a host of regulatory reforms to address the supervisory problem. Among the proposals were recommendations to improve the informal coordination of supervisory responsibilities across the Comptroller of the Currency, the Federal Deposit Insurance Corporation and the Fed. At the time, none of the agencies were willing to relinquish bank regulatory responsibilities. Later, during the Johnson Administration, Budget Director Kermit Gordon and Walter Heller, Chairman of the Council of Economic Advisers (CEA), suggested to the president that the only "permanent solution" to bank supervisory problems would be the creation of a single bank supervisory agency absorbing the authority of the Comptroller of the Currency, the Federal Deposit Insurance Corporation, and the Fed.[4]

From the time that the coordination problem first received widespread attention, the various agencies charged with bank supervision could not agree on the extent to which bank supervision could be undertaken independent of other financial regulatory responsibilities. The Board of Governors of the Federal Reserve System was particularly jealous of the bank supervisory authority of the Fed. Staff policy makers were concerned that zealous bank regulators could undo liberal monetary policies by enforcing strict standards for lending in recessions. A [Reserve Bank] presidents task force report described the relationship between supervision and monetary restraint:

> There can be no meaningful control of money, bank credit, or interest rates if the Federal Reserve is heavily involved in averting or containing bank crises or panics through relaxation of general monetary policies or specific assistance programs such as lender of last resort. It is evident that the strengths and weaknesses of banking organizations provides constraints within which monetary policy must operate.[5]

In later testimony to Congress on the Financial Reform of Act of 1976, Arthur Burns deplored the prospective consolidation of regulatory under a Federal Banking Commission. He argued that the segregation of bank supervisory tasks from monetary policy activities would complicate the tasks of monetary control. Bank examination data and information from member banks were described as vital for the administration of discount window lending and supervision of lending practices.[6] Seeking support from the administration to block regulatory consolidation, Burns claimed that actions by the Federal Banking Commission could "frustrate monetary policy and destroy the effectiveness of the Fed."[7]

Since the supervisory function is integral to the conduct of monetary policy by the Fed, the surrender of supervisory authority to another regulator would be unacceptable for Board members and Reserve Bank presidents. It would seem that greater supervisory and regulatory authority within the Fed would facilitate the conduct of monetary policy and increase the budget and operations of the central bank. The surprising outcome was that both members of the Board of Governors and the Reserve Bank presidents vigorously opposed the extension of Fed bank regulatory powers to nonmember banks.

Thrift Supervision and Monetary Policy

In 1974, the Federal Reserve System Conference of Bank Presidents authorized a Task Force Report on Bank Supervision and Regulation.[8] The Task Force was directed to report on the "ideal regulatory structure" without regard to the "political feasibility of implementing these recommendations."[9] If Fed decision makers were strictly interested in expanding functions and budgets, then the expected position of the Fed should be for the concentration of supervisory authority for all financial institutions under the Fed. The 1974 Task Force Report (and a parent Committee on Bank Supervision and Regulation) initially made such a recommendation. But Fed decision makers rejected the recommendations outright. Responses from the Reserve Bank presidents and the Board of Governors highlighted the perceived implications of these recommendations for the Fed. Prospective problems included increased congressional leverage over central bank activity and pressures from the various constituencies that were given preferential treatment by regulators of nonmember financial institutions, especially thrift regulators.

David Eastburn, President of the Federal Reserve Bank of Philadelphia, described his concerns to other Reserve Bank presidents:

> The proposal to place the full range of bank supervisory functions under the direction of the Federal Reserve might help monetary implementation in the short-run, but it could undermine it in the long run. As the Fed assumes more and more duties that have traditionally been subject to direct congressional supervision, its arguments for independence lose their force.[10]

Representatives of the Federal Reserve Bank of San Francisco also objected:

> Moreover, if it also absorbed the [Federal Home Loan Bank Board], the System would be subject to massive political pressures now diffused over several agencies. Interests of various industries and financial institutions would divert attention from monetary policy, or worse, force monetary policy to conform, for example, to the needs of the housing industry.[11]

The President of the Federal Reserve Bank of Chicago, Robert P. Mayo, also concluded that the establishment of bank supervisory authority inside the Fed would seriously threaten the future independence of the Fed. The General Counsel of the Federal Reserve Bank of Kansas City, while favoring consolidation of regulatory authority, identified several risks associated with the proposal including a possible General Accounting Office (GAO) audit, designation of Reserve Banks as government agencies, and surrender of the open market portfolio to effect a reduction in the national debt.[12]

The Board of Governors and Chairman Arthur Burns chose to oppose the concentration of bank supervisory authority under the Fed. Accepting broader regulatory authority could bring about incentives for representatives of home-builders and construction trades to seek preferential treatment from the Fed and for members of Congress to pressure the Fed to meet diverse credit needs within specific congressional districts. Opposition to broader regulatory authority was also consistent with other decisions by the Board of Governors and the Reserve Bank presidents to reject changes in central bank activities that would place the Fed under closer congressional scrutiny and amplify demands for allocation of capital across credit-dependent sectors of the economy.

Case 2: Resistance to Congressional Oversight

Fed decision makers have consistently opposed changes in the relationship between the Fed and the Congress that would either subject the Fed to the congressional appropriations process or subject Fed activities to any kind of oversight beyond occasional congressional hearings. House Concurrent Resolution 133, implemented in 1974, compelled a reluctant Board of Governors to semi-annually publish, explain and defend monetary aggregate growth targets before a congressional committee. Other congressional proposals to gain more information from the Fed have been described as failures. Scaggs (1983) argues that efforts to minimize the transmission of information about monetary policy targets and goals to Congress are generally consistent with the types of bureaucratic incentives suggested by neoclassical theories of (self-interested) bureaucratic behavior. Scaggs identifies three types of "disclosure-avoidance efforts" undertaken by the Board of Governors: resistance to Sunshine Laws, objections to GAO audits, and, finally, resistance to monetary targets. While these activities are generally consistent with bureaucratic budget maximization goals and the maintenance of informational asymmetries, internal deliberations within the Board of Governors reveal that the objections to oversight are typically wedded directly and explicitly to the broader idea of central bank autonomy from elected officials. Congressional oversight is not avoided in order to disguise true costs of agency activity or to discourage monitoring, but instead to restrict the ability of members of Congress to satisfy narrow demands for the allocation of capital.

General Accounting Office Audits

A 1933 amendment to the Federal Reserve Act specified that System income was not to be construed as appropriated funds or government money, effectively exempting the activities of the Fed from audit by the General Accounting Office.[13] Congressman Wright Patman led a series of efforts to update the Act and reintroduce GAO audits of financial transactions related to monetary policy. Under the direction of Patman, the Subcommittee on Domestic Finance (under the House Banking and Currency Committee) prepared a set of proposals for reform of the Fed in 1964. Provisions for GAO audit of the Fed were included in the proposals. Not unexpectedly, but to the surprise of Patman, the Johnson White House endorsed independence for the Fed at the same time that Patman was criticizing the decisions of the Fed. The Johnson White House statements endorsing independence were followed by positive Fed intervention in bond markets to stabilize long-term interest rates.[14] These events motivated observers at the time to conclude that the Fed acted at the behest of the administration (Beckhart 1972).

GAO audits were consistently opposed by both the White House and the Treasury before and after the Johnson Administration. The Department of the Treasury consistently rejected GAO audits of Fed activities as unnecessary and intrusive. Treasury Secretary George Humphrey defended independent credit and monetary policy during the Eisenhower administration. Douglas Dillon opposed audit proposals before the House Banking and Currency Committee during the Kennedy Administration. Henry Fowler adopted the same position during his tenure as Secretary of the Treasury under Lyndon Johnson. In 1975 six former Secretaries of the Treasury authored a letter to Henry Reuss opposing proposed GAO audits of transactions related to monetary policy; the audit proposals were described as a troublesome and inappropriate form of indirect congressional supervision.[15]

The Board of Governors of the Federal Reserve System also objected to audits supervised by Congress. Decision makers at the Fed perceived GAO audits as a first step toward subjecting Fed expenditures to the appropriations process. In 1973 Arthur Burns was specifically warned of the vulnerabilities of the Fed to strict audits:

> If Congressman Patman ever shifts his attention from baby-sitting fees and the like to our overall cost performance, I have no doubt that we will be placed under the appropriations process with full GAO audit.[16]

Senior staff members advised Burns in 1972 that the best way to resist GAO audit would be to contest public disclosure of confidential matters relating to foreign monetary relations, bank examination, and monetary policy details. Public disclosure would discourage frank exchange of information necessary to make policy choices. This attempt to claim special privileges for bank examination and transactions data was not effective. Elmer Staats, head of the GAO, informed Congressman Henry Reuss that the GAO routinely gained access to confidential material in the course of audits. He further suggested that he would interpret direction to audit the Fed to include limited authority to recommend improvements in operations or procedures.[17] When first directed to monitor the Fed, Staats even intended to audit the transactions in government securities undertaken in the context of open market operations.[18] In an effort to avert a mandatory and comprehensive audit of System activities by the GAO, the Fed voluntarily agreed in 1976 to allow the GAO to audit material related to the bank supervisory functions of the System.[19] The Fed was subjected to more comprehensive GAO audit before 1980.

Expenditure Ceilings

Senator William Proxmire proposed in 1975 that the Fed be subjected to an annual ceiling for expenditures. Board staff warned Chairman Burns that other agencies—such as the Federal Home Loan Bank Board—have simple appropriation ceilings that nevertheless entail review of budgets and appropriations by the Office of Management and Budget.[20] Reserve Bank presidents responded to the ceiling proposals with considerable alarm. Paul Volcker, then President of the Reserve Bank of New York, objected to annual expenditure ceilings as an instrument of political control:

> Individual Reserve Banks could be put in a position of agreeing to a particular policy or policy position in order to secure a larger authorization, and the System could, by virtue of similar pressures, be placed in a position of adopting certain policies or operating with funds limited to such a degree as to threaten the System's massive operations.[21]

David Eastburn, President of the Federal Reserve Bank of Philadelphia, concurred:

> This kind of surveillance would reduce the Fed's flexibility and open its operations to political considerations that could be seriously harmful to public welfare.

He concludes:

> This proposal, however, does suggest something for us to think about in making our own decisions about expenditures. The more

> we increase our spending in nonmonetary policy areas (for example, RCPC's, consumer affairs, etc.) the weaker becomes our case for being exempt from the usual congressional budgeting procedures. I believe it would be wise for us to rethink carefully the desirability—in light of the importance for monetary policy and the need for it to remain independent—of expanding our responsibilities into other areas. We may even want to suggest removing some of our existing responsibilities.[22]

The proposed legislation eventually passed as the Federal Reserve Reform Act of 1977, but the controversial provisions—annual expenditure ceilings and Senate confirmation of Reserve Bank presidents—were omitted from the final bill. It is clear the Reserve Bank presidents and members of the Board of Governors oppose any mechanism that may create incentives for members of Congress to induce the Fed to support particular sectors of the capital and money markets in the conduct of monetary policy.

Allocation of Capital and Central Bank Performance before 1980

Before 1980, capitulation to political demands for allocation of capital had particularly negative consequences for the central bank. Membership in the Fed was voluntary until 1980. Member banks submitted to reserve requirements and Fed supervision in exchange for access to the discount window and other Fed services. In practice, nearly all large bank financial institutions were members. Aggressive protection of particular economic sectors with monetary policy choices would have created incentives for the voluntary members of the Fed to exit the System. Thrift institutions and other financial institutions that concentrated on home mortgage lending were not members of the Fed. If monetary policy choices, as a result of demands from Congress, exclusively benefited home mortgage lenders, then the members of the Fed would be placed at a competitive disadvantage to nonmember financial institutions. Members would face constraints on business and other non-mortgage lending. Nonmembers would face few constraints. Central bank autonomy and discretion over the distribution of monetary restraint facilitated the retention of bank members in the Fed. Retention was a particularly salient goal for Fed decision makers who were concerned that member attrition threatened the base of reserves that the Fed used to make monetary policy (Meier 1985). The prospect of diminishing membership and tenuous control over bank reserves motivated central bank decision makers to resist congressional intervention in monetary policy and political allocation of credit through the central bank.[23] The membership problem would ultimately lead to Fed support for compulsory membership in the System and universal reserve requirements.

AUTONOMY AND INSTITUTIONAL CHANGE

Explanations of monetary policy choices have typically appealed to either the parametric budget maximizing behavior of public sector bureaucrats or to the transmission of external demands from elected officials to bureaucratic subordinates. Each of these explanations share a conspicuous omission of the strategies of bureaucratic agents. Neoclassical bureaucrats maximize revenues within a fixed set of institutional constraints; mechanistic agents are assumed to function within constraints engineered by political principals. The theory of bureau behavior offered by both the neoclassical economic model and the hierarchical control model discounts institutional change as an important source of bureau discretion and autonomy. The omission of strategies and actions of bureaucratic agents is a shortcoming of these models: agency decision makers can manipulate institutions to subvert political controls by transforming the "rules of the game" originally set out by political principals.

Lombra (1988) makes the case that some Fed activities—such as the use of multiple intermediate targets for policy goals—are specifically intended to maximize autonomy in the day-to-day conduct of monetary policy. The Fed relies on what Arthur Burns described as a "menu of aggregates" to report System objectives and evaluate System performance. Since multiple aggregate targets are only marginally costly to implement, it is difficult to assess how central bank policy makers sacrifice resources or prestige in order to maximize autonomy. A strong claim can be made about the preferences of Fed decision makers if there are specific instances where decision makers at the Fed bear costs in order to gain autonomy. Resistance of central bankers to greater bank regulatory authority in the 1970s represents such a case. A series of choices made within the Fed in the early 1970s blocked a wide extension of the powers and activities of the central bank. Decisions to oppose legislation incorporating new bank supervisory and regulatory responsibilities in the Federal Reserve Act was tantamount to the rejection of greater operating budgets, more staff and greater authority. The perceived trade-off within the Fed was between greater resources and increased attention from Congress and lobbyists promoting the interests of affected financial institutions. Reserve Bank presidents were particularly vigorous opponents to regulatory innovations.

Existing theories of bureaucratic behavior link purposeful decisions of bureaucrats to either increasing revenue from regulatory activity or increasing monitoring costs of sponsoring agencies. An alternative set of motivations, which can plausibly be attributed to decision makers in the Fed, explains changes in monetary policy institutions. Postwar changes in central banking practice, described in the next three chapters of the book, are intentionally designed to enhance central bank autonomy. Central bankers in the United States act in ways consistent with the maintenance of central bank autonomy and independence from political oversight. Central bankers select the set of instruments used to implement monetary policy in order to maximize autonomy. Choices by Fed decision makers minimize intervention from both outside of government and within government. The strategic choices of these central bankers are intended to prevent the interests of particular economic sectors from dominating monetary policy, either by direct influence of representatives of particular sectors or by indirect pressure from elected officials. The procedural changes undertaken to maintain autonomy have consequences that extend beyond the representation of particular economic sectors in the formulation of monetary policy. The strategic choices affect the set of options available to members of Congress and White House. Institutional changes at the central bank have important consequences for the ability of political actors to pursue a variety of ideological and electoral goals which they value. The next three chapters reveal how monetary policy institutions were updated by Fed decision makers and how decision makers balanced strategic and technical objectives over time. Each set of instruments, reserve requirements, open market transactions, and selective controls is updated consistent with the maintenance and expansion of Fed autonomy.

NOTES

1. Sociological approaches to the study of hierarchy and bureaucracy have also suggested that discretion or autonomy is an important incentive for agents and workers. Rather than as a means to some end, the pursuit of discretion in the selection of tasks and goals has been identified as an important incentive for agents in recent work on private industrial organization and hierarchies, as well as a primary result of early work on industrial bureaucracy. (Gouldner 1954, Akerlof 1982).

2. Appendix A. "Federal Reserve Balance Sheet and Reserve Equation." *Federal Reserve System: Purposes and Functions.* Washington D.C.: Board of Governors of the Federal Reserve System. 1994.

3. Reserve requirements and membership attrition are described in detail in Chapter 3.

4. Memo. Kermit Gordon and Walter Heller to The President. 28 Feb 1964. Folder: *FI2. Banks—Banking.* FI Series. Box #13. Papers of Lyndon Baines Johnson. Lyndon Baines Johnson Library.

5. Report. Task Force for Reforming the Structure of Regulatory Agencies Supervising Banking Organizations and Related Depository Institutions. 25 Sep 1974. Folder: *Bank Regulatory Reform: October, 1974.* Papers of Arthur Burns. Gerald R. Ford Library.

6. Statement of Arthur Burns before the Subcommittee on Financial Institutions Supervision, Regulation and Insurance. House Banking Committee. 18 March 1976. Folder: *FG 33-4. House Committee—Banking.* Box #122. White House Central Files. Gerald R. Ford Library.

7. Memo. Chairman Burns to CEA Chairman Greenspan. 8 March 1976. Folder: *FO 6-1. Economic Summit Conference.* Box #32. White House Central Files. Gerald R. Ford Library.

8. The official title of the investigating body was the Task Force for Reforming the Structure of Regulatory Agencies Supervising Banking Organizations and Related Depository Institutions.

9. Letter. Alfred Hayes, President, Federal Reserve Bank of New York, to Arthur Burns. 10 Oct 1974. Folder: *Bank Regulatory Reform: October, 1974.* Papers of Arthur Burns. Gerald R. Ford Library.

10. Letter. David Eastburn, President, Federal Reserve Bank of Philadelphia to Alfred Hayes, President, Federal Reserve Bank of New York. 1 Oct 1974. Folder: *Bank Regulatory Reform: October, 1974.* Box #B7. Papers of Arthur Burns. Gerald R. Ford Library.

11. Comments. Federal Reserve Bank of San Francisco. Forwarded to Alfred Hayes, President of the Federal Reserve Bank of New York. 1 Oct

1974. Folder: *Bank Regulatory Reform: October, 1974.* Box #B7. Papers of Arthur Burns. Gerald R. Ford Library.

12. Letter. Roger Guffey, Senior Vice President and General Counsel, Federal Reserve Bank of Kansas City, to Arthur Burns. Folder: *Bank Regulatory Reform: August-September, 1974.* Box #B7. Papers of Arthur Burns. Gerald R. Ford Library.

13. Memo. P.D. Ring to Chairman Burns. 27 September 1973. Folder: *GAO Audit.* October 1-10, 1973. Box #B50. Papers of Arthur Burns. Gerald R Ford Library.

14. Memo. Heller to Johnson. 5 August 1964. Folder: *FG 233. Federal Reserve System. EX.* White House Central Files. Lyndon Baines Johnson Library. (Also the 13 August 1964 letter in the same location.) See the Federal Reserve Bulletin March, 1965 for a summary of monthly open market purchases for calendar year 1964.

15. Letter. Joseph Barr to Henry Reuss. 16 August 1975. Folder: *Federal Reserve System, Reform of.* Box #B42. Papers of Arthur Burns. Gerald R. Ford Library.

16. Memo. James McIntosh to Arthur Burns. 12 February 1973. Folder: *Federal Reserve System Expenses, 1973-4.* Box #B42. Papers of Arthur Burns. Gerald R. Ford Library.

17. Letter. Elmer Staats to Henry Reuss. 27 May 1975. Folder: *GAO Audit. June, 1975.* Box # B51. Papers of Arthur Burns. Gerald R. Ford Library.

18. Letter. Elmer Staats to Representative Ashley. 7 March 1974. Folder: *GAO Audit. January-April, 1974.* Box #B51. Papers of Arthur Burns. Gerald R. Ford Library.

19. Letter. Arthur Burns to Elmer Staats. 5 May 1976. Folder: *General Accounting Office, 1976.* Box #B50. Papers of Arthur Burns. Gerald R. Ford Library.

20. Memo. E.T. Mulrenin to John Denkler. 14 August 1975. Folder: *Federal Reserve System, Reform of (2).* Box #B42. Papers of Arthur Burns. Gerald R. Ford Library.

21. Letter. Paul Volcker, President of the Federal Reserve Bank of New York, to the Board of Governors of the Federal Reserve System. 15 August 1975. Folder: *Federal Reserve System, Reform of (1).* Box #B42. Papers of Arthur Burns. Gerald R. Ford Library.

22. Letter. David Eastburn, President of the Federal Reserve Bank of Philadelphia, to the Board of Governors of the Federal Reserve System. 15

August 1975. Folder: *Federal Reserve System, Reform of (1)*. Box #B42. Papers of Arthur Burns. Gerald R. Ford Library.

23. Memo. Division of Research and Statistics to the Board of Governors. 23 July 1974. Folder: *Reuss, Henry. January, 1972—January, 1975*. Congressional Correspondence. Box #O16. Papers of Arthur Burns. Gerald R. Ford Library.

CHAPTER 3

Reserve Requirements and the Distribution of Monetary Restraint

Reserve requirements specify the percentage of commercial bank liabilities that must be held at the Federal Reserve regional banks in order to meet demands of depositors or other claims against commercial banks. The requirements obligate a financial institution to place funds in a reserve account at a regional Federal Reserve Bank. Since the reserve accounts yield no interest, financial institutions realize no return on bank assets that serve as reserves. Any profits generated by the investment of the contents of these reserve accounts in government securities is held by the Fed, so reserve requirements redistribute revenue from commercial banks to the regional Federal Reserve Banks. Required reserves therefore function as an implicit tax on the financial institutions to which they apply.

Studies of monetary policy outcomes by political scientists and political economists typically have as a singular focus the extent to which central bank policies expand or contract the aggregate supply of credit and money available to finance economic activity. Indicators of expansion and contraction include aggregate nonborrowed commercial bank reserves, the federal funds rate, and the narrow money aggregate (M1). In this context, reserve requirements are either high (meaning tighter money) or low (meaning easier money). Little attention is given to variation in the scope and definition of required reserves. This omission is surprising given the distributive implications of changes in reserve requirements. Since the structure of reserve requirements determines the distribution of an implicit tax burden across types and classes of financial institutions, changes in reserve requirements are ultimately redistributive choices. It would seem to matter to both commercial bankers and elected officials whether or not, for instance, bank holdings other than deposits at a Federal Reserve Bank can be counted as cash reserves. Banks that routinely hold large amounts of vault cash, at one time characteristic of rural banks, would be disadvantaged if those assets could not be counted as reserves. Since important redistributive effects accompany changes in reserve requirements, these changes should attract considerable attention from members of Congress. Reserve requirements determine what types of financial institutions are most directly affected by monetary restraint and what types of borrowers face the dearest interest rate premiums when monetary policy is tightened. Elected officials are likely to have preferences over how monetary policy is distributed across the economy, so reserve requirements could be a focus of efforts by elected officials to influence monetary policy outcomes. Fed policy makers, reflecting a systematic strategy of avoiding congressional intervention in monetary policy choices, consistently rely on indirect rules and administrative updates (rather than statutory instructions) to manage reserve requirements.

MANAGEMENT AND REFORM OF THE RESERVE REQUIREMENT INSTRUMENT

Under the Federal Reserve Act, members of Congress set the ceiling and floor for the reserve requirements administered by the Board of Governors of the Federal Reserve System. The statutory minimum and maximum were fixed for most classes of banks from 1935 until 1959, and then revised downward. For the purposes of administering reserve requirements, the Federal Reserve Act specified three geographic classes of bank financial institutions, each with unique reserve requirements: central reserve city banks, reserve city banks, and country banks. In the thirty-five year period from the creation of the Fed until 1948, reserve requirements applied to central city banks were changed only eight times: raised four times and lowered four times. In the same period, reserve requirements were changed five times for country banks and city banks. Required reserves were first implemented at the statutory minimum in June 1917 and reached the statutory maximum in November 1941.

Reserve requirements were frequently used as an instrument of monetary policy after 1948. Between 1948 and 1978, reserve requirements were raised or lowered nearly twenty seven times for the largest banks (ten times during the Truman Administration alone). The increasing frequency of use was coupled with an increasingly critical assessment of the selective and distributive effects of the reserve requirement instrument. Thomas McCabe, Chairman of the Board of Governors of the Federal Reserve System, questioned the usefulness of the blunt reserve requirement instrument in 1950. At the time, reserve requirements failed to allow policy makers to discriminate across classes of banks or banks with different portfolios:

> One of the disadvantages of an increase in reserve requirements is its unselective application to banks. It affects all banks alike in relation to their respective deposits without regard to the nature of their assets or their current credit policies. In contrast, open market operations exert their influence indirectly through the money market without an obvious and direct influence upon commercial banks.[1]

Later, during the tenure of Chairman William Martin, the Board of Governors of the Federal Reserve System engaged in a systematic effort to rehabilitate the reserve requirement instrument. The object of the reform was to target the effects of changes in required reserves to specific types of financial institutions. To carry out this reform the Board of Governors, and occasionally Congress, were confronted with three types of questions about the distribution of reserves and the treatment of particular types of financial institutions by the Fed.

1. The Scope of Required Reserves. Should reserve requirements be designed to treat all functional types of financial institutions as identical? More narrowly, should all depository institutions be subject to reserve requirements?

2. Differentiation by Size. Administrative changes in 1966 substituted size criteria for the geographic criteria used to group bank financial institutions for the purpose of administering reserve requirements. Should reserve requirements be designed to treat all sizes of financial institutions as identical?

3. Differentiation by Portfolio. Should reserve requirements be designed to treat all banks equally, regardless of the composition of bank portfolios (assets and liabilities)? Or should reserve requirements encourage banks to lengthen the maturity of liabilities or to hold, for instance, home mortgages as assets?

Each of these questions raises both technical and distributive issues. The technical problem is precision. Direct regulation of individual bank reserves abets precise control over the aggregate level of reserves and, ultimately, the money supply. Broad and unselective reserve requirements are equitable and indirect, but foreclose precise control over aggregate reserves levels. The distributive problem is related to the heterogeneity of bank financial institutions. Bank portfolios vary in ways that affect the impact of reserve requirements on bank lending and financing activity. Large banks are not burdened by reserve requirements in the same way that small banks are burdened. Banks that hold many less liquid assets such as home mortgages or long-term debt instruments (notably, municipal bonds) are more vulnerable to changes in reserve requirements than banks that hold mostly short-term debt instruments (Treasury bills or short-term business loans). Increasing reserve requirements not only reduces aggregate lending and financial activity, but disproportionately affects lending to home owners and state and local government.

Each of the three mechanisms used to adjust the distribution of the reserve burden (scope, size, and portfolio) has specific effects on the distribution of the burdens of monetary restraint across financial institutions and borrowers. Members of Congress and staff at the White House have been effectively disengaged from debate and consideration of alternative reserve requirements and alternative redistributive choices. Institutional choices of decision makers in the Fed have reinforced the idea that reserve requirements are unselective and indirect, rather than direct and consequential tools for the distribution of the costs of monetary restraint. Each adjustment mechanism (scope, size, and portfolio) was updated between 1948 and 1980. Each update reinforces central bank autonomy.

The Scope of the Reserve Requirement

The Membership Problem.

Since reserve requirements impose costs (an implicit tax) on the voluntary members of the Fed, high reserve requirements reduce the number of financial institutions that choose to join. Declining membership then reduces the size of the pool of reserves that the Fed relies upon to implement monetary policy.[2] During the 1970s, the Board of Governors of the Fed consistently maintained that membership attrition undermined the precision of monetary control exercised by the System. A staff presentation to the Board of Governors in March 1973 advocated the use of strict reserve requirements to curtail bank lending and reduce the growth rate of the money aggregates. The report noted that reserve regulation directly reduced bank liquidity and carried a strong announcement effect. The staff report warned, however, that a major disadvantage was the problem of System membership. Voluntary nonmember compliance would be essential for bank lending to be contained.[3] The Federal Reserve Bank of New York actually recommended that reserve requirement choices be determined by potential effects on membership, rather than objectives related to monetary control.

Membership problems frequently restricted the use of reserve requirements to affect monetary policy goals between 1950 and 1978. System decision makers were particularly reluctant to enact onerous reserve requirements in periods of vigorous monetary expansion. Since changes in reserve requirements affect only banks that choose to be members of the Fed, commercial banks could withdraw from the Fed in periods of monetary restraint. The banks would then be subjected only to the less demanding reserve requirements of state regulators or, depending on the type of bank, to the reserve requirements specified by other federal bank regulatory agencies. This membership problem had an unambiguous effect on the monetary policy choices of the Board of Governors. Reserve requirements on small banks were not increased at all between February 1951 and November 1960. Required reserves were lowered three times in the same period. (See Figure 2 for the specific frequency of changes in required reserves.) In practice, membership attrition was a serious constraint upon monetary policy choices.

A Statutory Solution: Universal Reserve Requirements

After World War II, two consecutive Chairmen of the Board of Governors of the Federal Reserve System (Marriner Eccles and Thomas McCabe) advocated extension of limited reserve requirements to all financial institutions. The banking community, including the American Bankers Association (ABA), strongly objected to the extension of reserve requirements to nonmember banks. It was feared that extension of reserve requirements to all financial institutions

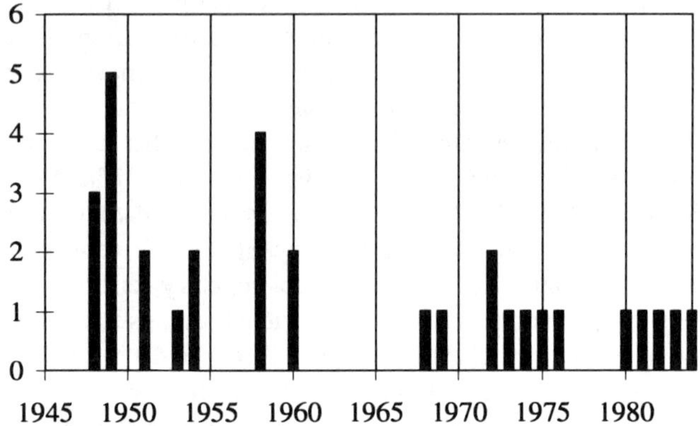

Figure 2
Frequency of changes in the definition or level of the reserve requirement (1945-1985).

Source: Annual Report of the Board of Governors of the Federal Reserve System, Various Years.

would undermine the power of state regulators and vitiate the dual banking system.[4] The preservation of the dual banking system—intended to encourage innovation and market entry—motivated opponents of universal reserve requirements to block the extension of reserve requirements into the early 1970s.[5]

Despite opposition from small banks, policy makers in the Fed proposed the extension of reserve requirements to nonmember financial institutions as part of several prospective reforms of System procedures. Universal reserve requirements were recommended in congressional reports issued by the Douglas Committee (1950) and the Patman Committee (1952), by external commissions such as the Commission on Money and Credit (1960) and the Hunt Commission (1973), and explicitly endorsed by the Board of Governors of the Federal Reserve System in 1967[6],and 1974.[7] To address the problem of member attrition, Arthur Burns requested that the Nixon CEA advocate extension of reserve requirements and discount borrowing privileges to all depository institutions.[8] The result of this request was a joint report by Fed staff and CEA staff "incorporating the objectives of Chairman Burns with respect to monetary control and those of Chairman Stein with respect to preservation of the dual banking system".[9] Regulators of nonmember banks, notably the Conference of State Bank Supervisors, opposed the recommendations.[10] The Conference feared broader authority for the Board of Governors would centralize credit allocation in the Fed. Congress did not act upon the joint recommendations.

Reserve requirements were finally extended to nonmember financial institutions with the passage of DIDMCA. One important reason for the shift from voluntary membership to universal application was the demands of large commercial banks (Meier 1985). The ABA, in particular, supported the 1980 extension of reserve requirements. As technological innovations permitted savings and loans and other depository institutions to offer services similar to commercial bank checking accounts, high reserve requirements placed all commercial banks at a competitive disadvantage to nonmember financial institutions. Universal reserve requirements could eliminate these competitive disadvantages. Universal reserve requirements would benefit commercial bank members of the Fed relative to nonmember financial institutions, especially thrifts.

The extension of reserve requirements to all financial institutions may be the most important postwar change in the administration of reserve requirements. DIDMCA extended the reserve requirements of the Fed to all depository institutions: commercial banks, mutual savings banks, savings and loan associations, credit unions, and Edge Act corporations. Speculation about the ultimate effects of the 1980 Act has motivated some of the most vocal criticisms of the Fed and the oversight of monetary policy by elected officials. The extension of reserve requirements was described by William Greider as a technical deception of Congress by the Fed:

> The imposition of universal reserve requirements was presented to Congress as an arcane question of monetary management, the sort of issue few members of Congress cared much about or understood. In reality, the Fed membership issue was a political question, only marginally relevant to economics. (Greider 1987, 155)

Greider concludes that the 1980 extension of reserve requirements to all financial institutions created incredible wealth for member banks, especially large commercial banks. Since reserve requirements were extended to all financial institutions and the reserves base expanded, reserve requirements on member banks could be lowered without jeopardizing monetary control. The lower reserve requirement increased member bank earning assets by nearly 14 billion dollars—a windfall of income equivalent to over 1 billion dollars a year if invested in government securities at prevailing interest rates (Greider 1987). Greider claims that the change in reserve requirements was a benefit intended to stabilize and reward the powerful political constituents of the Fed: large commercial banks. It is not at all clear that members of Congress were deceived or misled about the economic and distributive effects of the changes. Members of Congress were informed of the specific economic benefits that would accrue to large banks in their home districts (Greider 1987,162).

The net effect of the statutory change (across all financial institutions) was to only temporarily ease the implicit tax imposed by the Fed on banks. Required reserves increased by nearly fifty percent between 1984 and 1988. The level of required reserves is displayed in Figure 3, below. Current levels remain well under the real levels observed in the early 1970s and very close to the real levels observed when DIDMCA was passed.

Central bank discretion under the new rules

The transition to universal membership and the magnitude of real required reserves would be unremarkable if reserve requirements imposed no costs on financial institutions. Reserve requirements are instead a political liability for central bank decision makers. Raising reserve requirements—equivalent to placing prospective commercial bank assets at a Federal Reserve Bank—imposes costs on financial institutions. Reducing reserve requirements—returning commercial bank assets for bank use—increases financing costs for the Treasury and benefits financial institutions. The Fed rebates the majority of the interest payments received from Treasury, so high reserve requirements decrease financing costs. Since reductions in reserve requirements are consistent with efforts to stimulate the economy, economic benefits are typically directed to financial institutions during periods of economic recession. This type of redistribution is a liability

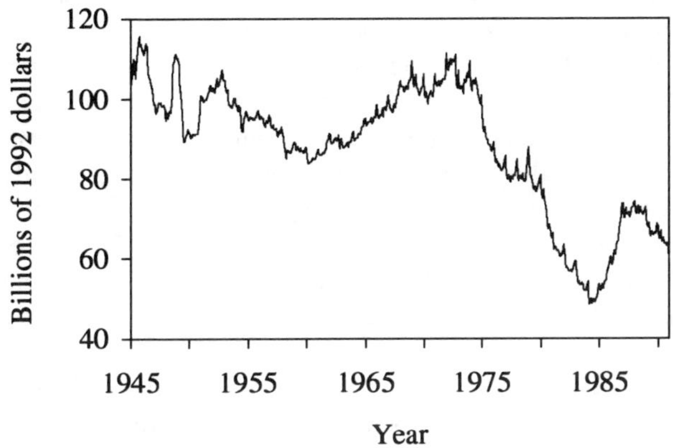

Figure 3
Required reserves, adjusted for inflation (1945-1990) [not seasonally adjusted].

Source: Federal Reserve Economic Data, Federal Reserve Bank of St. Louis.

for Fed decision makers. Evaluating prospective changes in reserve requirements in early 1975, Fed staff projected that for each $100 million dollars in reserves released to the banking system the Treasury would expend (after tax adjustments) an additional $3.2 million in interest payments on government securities held by commercial banks.[11] Fed staff are therefore reluctant to recommend the use of reserve requirements as a variable instrument, particularly when other policy objectives may be affected:

> Use of the reserve requirement device may be limited effectively by the political sensitivity of an action which transfers earning assets from the Federal Reserve to commercial banks. To the extent this is so, an across-the-board cut now could impinge on the Board's ability to effect a structural reform in reserve requirements as discussed in recent months.[12]

Universal requirements may enhance monetary control and could increase System revenue—desirable outcomes for decision makers in the Fed. But at the same time universal requirements increase the probability of resistance to changes in the structure of reserve requirements. Universal requirements invite political opposition by eliminating the traditional exit option under voluntary membership. An increase in reserve requirements may bring about the same type of opposition from home builders as the prospective Fed supervisory responsibilities described in Chapter 2. High reserve requirements on thrifts could motivate home builders to challenge Fed monetary policy choices.

The new universal rules appear to be specifically designed to minimize political opposition: phase-in of required reserves took place over eight years, most differential reserve requirements were eliminated, and a new mechanism automatically adjusts the deposit interval that graduates required reserves according to size of deposits. Refinements to the requirements specified in the Garn-St Germain Depository Institutions Act of 1982 required a discrete amount of bank liabilities to be subjected to a zero percent reserve requirement. (The Annual Report of the Board of Governors for 1985 describes the new reserve arrangements in detail.)

The extension of reserve requirements removes a constraint on Fed activity (the membership problem) that has been used in the past to oppose proposals to compel commercial banks to support particular economic sectors. Voluntary membership was a persistent obstacle to the use of reserve requirements intended to influence the lending practices of commercial banks. If reserve requirements were too burdensome, then banks could defect from the Fed. The Board of Governors warned members of Congress considering new reserve requirements that the costs of declining membership could outweigh the benefits of highly selective reserve requirements. Absent the problem of membership, what prevents Congress from compelling the Fed to use reserve requirements to regulate bank lending behavior? Congress could respond to the incentives created by DIDMCA by broadening the scope of required reserves to protect particular economic sectors (especially construction and trades). Or Congress could narrow the effects of required reserves to minimize the impact of monetary policy choices on the asset and liability portfolios of financial institutions, consistent with other types of deregulation. Past experience has made the Board of Governors reluctant to place these distributive choices at the discretion of Congress.

THE SMALL BANK / LARGE BANK PROBLEM

The Vault Cash Act (1959)

Specific congressional direction and intervention in the stipulation of reserve requirements is rare. The Federal Reserve Act specifies the minimum and maximum percentage of reserves that can be held at the regional Reserve Banks. Most changes in the structure of reserve requirements require only administrative action by the Board of Governors of the Federal Reserve System. Congressional attention is only required when specific components of the Federal Reserve Act require revision. The Board of Governors requested that Congress amend the Federal Reserve Act in 1959 in order to allow banks to count vault cash as reserves against liabilities. The accounting change was particularly beneficial to small, country banks that hold large amounts of vault cash. The Board of Governors argued that these changes were necessary to eliminate competitive inequities between country banks and similarly sized competitor banks in large cities. Congressional action on the proposal was delayed by a narrow group of opponents in the House of Representatives including Wright Patman. Patman characterized the bill as a massive give away of government securities—nearly $15 billion dollars.[13] In practice, cash used to satisfy reserve requirements is not held by the Fed at the Reserve Banks but instead invested in government securities and other secure short-term money market instruments (allowing the Fed to finance day-to-day operations with the interest income). A reduction in the reserves held at the Reserve Banks implied that the Fed must sell government securities and credit the reserve accounts of country banks. The country banks could then purchase short-term government securities with the excess reserves. The administrative changes essentially transferred $15 billion in government securities from the Fed portfolio to the country banks. Opposition to this type of redistribution made passage of the Vault Cash Act unexpectedly contentious and embarrassed representatives of the Fed.

In the 1970s staff members of the Board of Governors used the 1959 experience to warn current members of the Board of Governors against attempting to disguise distributive actions as strictly administrative changes in Fed policy.[14] During the tenure of Arthur Burns, the Board of Governors studied and implemented a variety of changes in reserve requirements that distributed the burdens of monetary restraint in fairly specific ways. The distributive effects were neither advertised for members of Congress nor explicitly described in policy deliberations in the FOMC.

Graduated Reserve Requirements (1972)

Graduated reserve requirements allow banks of different size to hold a different proportion of bank liabilities in reserve. Efforts by the Board of Governors to formally move toward graduated reserve requirements after World War II were at first unsuccessful. The ABA and the Commission on Money and Credit (sponsored by the Eisenhower Administration) advocated uniform reserve requirements. The persistence of uniform reserve requirements (except for the geographic differentiation between city banks and country banks) unambiguously favored large banks. Large banks typically own a large pool of short-term debt that can be used to manage reserve requirements. Smaller banks are more likely to sell long-term assets to meet reserves shortfalls. The possibility of a graduated reserves structure was revisited during the debate over financial regulation in the Kennedy Administration. The Report of the Committee on Financial Institutions prepared for President Kennedy in 1963 formally recommended the adoption of graduated reserve requirements (Carson 1966). The absence of a clear consensus among legislators about the desirability of statutory changes necessary to implement the recommendations of the Kennedy Report foreclosed any immediate progress toward graduated reserves.

The Board of Governors of the Federal Reserve System requested legislative authority to expand and revise reserve requirements in 1971, but Board staff elected to independently undertake the changes using updates to administrative rules. Robert Holland, the Executive Director of the Board of Governors, and Robert Cardon recommended administrative changes in the structure of reserve requirements, rather than statutory changes to the Federal Reserve Act. Cardon explains the legislative dilemma:

> The main obstacle to the enactment of the Board's legislative proposals on reserve requirements is that the Board is asking the

> Congress to choose between two unpalatable alternatives. Reserve requirements cannot be changed without reducing earnings of some banks or cutting Treasury receipts.
>
> . . . Mr. Patman and others in Congress are inclined to look through the abstractions and generalities offered in support of bills, to discover who will benefit or suffer, and why.[15]

In an effort to encourage small banks to remain in the Fed, graduated reserve requirements were implemented in 1972. The Board of Governors approved changes in Regulation D, Reserve Requirements, that changed the distribution of reserve requirements across member banks to favor smaller banks. The administrative changes in the structure of reserve requirements compelled a number of large bank financial institutions to withdraw from the Fed. Despite the new graduated structure, the Board of Governors lowered required reserves throughout the 1970s as members (especially small banks) continued to withdraw from the Fed.

COMMERCIAL BANK LENDING PRACTICES AND THE RESERVE REQUIREMENT

Differential Reserve Requirements

Banks seek funds to finance lending activity from a variety of sources: demand deposit accounts, certificates of deposit, asset sales, and conventional debt instruments. By placing high reserve requirements on one source of funds (and low reserve requirements on alternatives), the Fed can discourage the use of particular sources of funds to finance lending activity by commercial banks. Reserves cannot be loaned to bank customers, so any sources of funds that require high reserves are unattractive for lenders. For instance, if 12 percent of all funds obtained from the issue of commercial paper by banks were to held in reserve but only 8 percent of all funds obtained from the sale of Certificates of Deposit were held in reserve, banks are discouraged from using commercial paper to raise funds. These types of *differential* reserve requirements on bank liabilities create specific incentives for banks to adjust the composition of the bank portfolio of liabilities and assets. Banks are encouraged to accept no more high-reserve liabilities and to attract low-reserve liabilities. Decision makers in the Fed considered aggressive extension of this mechanism to regulate commercial bank lending practices in the 1970s.[16] Differential reserve requirements were used in the 1970s to encourage banks to lengthen the maturities of their portfolios, to limit bank use of commercial paper, and to encourage banks to retain Euro-dollar liabilities.[17]

Limiting Placement of Commercial Paper

In early 1970, the staff at the Fed considered taking specific steps to limit and regulate the issue of commercial paper by bank financial institutions.

> On balance, it would seem best at this time to have a small differential reserve requirement on commercial paper as compared with CDs, to indicate that the Board considers commercial paper to be a riskier and less desirable means of banks' raising funds.[18]

The ABA, among others, opposed the new requirements. The ABA position was that in the absence of commercial paper sources of funds, banks must sell assets such as government securities to meet reserve requirements and loan demands. A. W. Clausen, President of the Bank of America, explained commercial bank objections to Arthur Burns:

> The use of the Credit Control Act of 1969 to impose reserve requirements on commercial paper is an unprecedented move. It raises questions about the propriety of applying reserves to asset sales of an outright, nonrecourse nature. Presumably the door is now open to the imposition of reserves on assets of any type.[19]

In August 1970, the Board of Governors announced new reserve requirements against funds obtained through the issue of commercial paper by bank affiliates. Beneficial distributive effects of the 1970 reforms were specifically discussed by Board staff:

> In particular, banks that do not rely on bank-related commercial paper as a source of funds and banks that obtain a relatively large share of their funds from time deposits would be favored. Since such banks are typically located outside of money centers, this redistributional effect would tend to encourage a different mix in bank credit extensions with more funds being provided for

> municipal bond investments and mortgage loans, and less to loans for larger business.[20]

The Board explicitly encouraged banks that benefited from the reduction of reserve requirements against time deposits to use a "sizable share" of the new reserves to fund home mortgages and state and local government finance.[21]

This type of distributive action is not unusual. Observers of central bank activity that focus exclusively on the macroeconomic implications of central bank activity might dismiss this type of reform as trivial. The aggregate effect is simply to shift capital from one sector to another without increasing or decreasing the aggregate level of money in financial markets. The distributive implications are not so trivial. Decision makers in the Fed expected the change in reserve requirements to lower the cost of capital for local governments and home owners, while increasing the costs of capital for big business.

During the 1970s, Fed decision makers routinely relied on the distributive effects of changes in required reserves to meet particular objectives of monetary and credit policy. An August 1973 adjustment in the structure of reserve requirements was optimistically described by Board staff as a precise and selective instrument:

> A further 3 percentage point increase in the marginal reserve requirements on large CDs and related domestic bank instruments could be viewed as a selective monetary tool to further restrain expansion in CDs and business loans. It could be taken, in other words, as an effort at tilting the direction of monetary restraint more toward business borrowing.[22]

Similarly, an October 1974 reduction in reserve requirements was endorsed by Board staff because (among other reasons) the reduction shifted credit toward business, housing, and consumer loans.[23]

Liability Management and Congressional Action

One consequence of the refinements in administration of reserve requirements was increasing complexity in the regulations. For instance, in November 1974 the Fed announced that reserve requirements were increasing for time deposits with a maturity of four months or less, decreasing for longer time deposits, decreasing for demand deposits over $400 million, and eliminated for large Certificates of Deposits maturing in less than four months. Decision makers in the Fed used adjustments in the reserve requirement instrument to indirectly influence the lending practices of commercial banks, without resorting to direct regulation. Since the decision makers had a fairly good idea of what types of banks would be encouraged to loan more and what types of banks would be encouraged to slow lending under the new set of requirements, Fed policy makers could use the reserve rules to encourage growth of lending to particular economic sectors and slow the growth of lending to other sectors.

Liability management goals were clearly integrated into the reserve requirement instrument during the 1970s. This selective instrument is narrowly focused on member bank liability management practices and only indirectly linked to bank lending practices. If the strategic imperative of a central banker is to retain the discretion to influence the distribution of credit indirectly, then liability management incentives are an appealing compromise between uniform reserve requirements and direct regulation of lending practices. Liability management incentives sacrifice some precision of control over allocation of capital since banks are free to vary assets (lending) despite reserves incentives. Precise control over the distribution of monetary restraint using the reserve requirement instrument can only be achieved by linking reserve requirements to the composition of bank assets. In exchange for the loss of precision, central bankers gain some freedom from statutory constraints and political intervention that would inevitably accompany direct links between reserve requirements and bank assets. Differential reserve requirements on bank liabilities do not create specific opportunities for members of Congress to direct credit and capital to particular economic sectors. Regulating the types of assets that banks acquire (mortgages, business loans, or consumer debt) abets precise control over the distribution of monetary restraint and exuberance, but invites supervision and oversight from Congress.

SUPPLEMENTARY RESERVE REQUIREMENTS

Banks acquire consumer debt, government debt, and business debt as assets. As instruments of monetary control, reserve requirements can be used to directly affect the composition of assets held in commercial bank portfolios. Two particular policy goals have motivated consideration of reserve requirements applied to assets: first, to induce banks to buy and hold government securities and, second, to induce banks to increase lending to particular sectors (typically state and local government or home buyers). This type of regulation of banks assets requires the central bank to attach specific reserve requirements to particular bank assets (government securities, home mortgages, business loans) rather than basing reserve levels on bank liabilities (contents of checking and savings accounts). Differential reserves on bank assets create incentives for bank lenders to adjust the contents of the portfolio of bank assets to minimize required reserves. Low reserve requirements on home mortgages, for instance, would encourage banks to buy and hold home mortgages and lower the cost of credit for mortgages.

The link between commercial bank asset portfolio decisions and political objectives of elected officials should be clear: if commercial banks are given incentives to hold a number of home mortgages as assets, then more and cheaper capital will be available to potential home buyers. The opposite is also true. If commercial banks choose to sell mortgages, then—all other things being equal—mortgage interest rates will rise. Similarly, if commercial banks hold a number of government securities, debt financing is less expensive for the federal government. Any central bank decision that encourages banks to hold and buy a particular class of assets benefits a particular group of borrowers.

Without resorting to direct regulation of reserves and differential reserves applied to bank assets, the Board of Governors of the Federal Reserve System can affect bank decisions about asset sales by introducing *supplementary reserve requirements.* Supplemental reserve requirements allow banks to count particular classes of assets as reserves, equivalent to vault cash or holdings at the regional Reserve Bank. If a class of assets can be counted as reserves, then the bank faces strong incentives to acquire more of these reserve-eligible assets and to sell assets that are not reserve-eligible. Two sets of supplemental reserve requirements have been proposed for incorporation into the Federal Reserve Act. Members of Congress have proposed supplementary reserve requirements to encourage the purchase of government securities and to channel credit to particular sectors of the economy. Neither proposal has been implemented. Both proposals implicate the central bank directly in the political process of credit allocation. Debate over the utility of the supplemental reserves requirements has generated some of the most frank and interesting debate over the role of the central bank in capital and money markets.

Supplemental reserves in the form of government securities

Supplemental reserve requirements allowing banks to hold government securities as reserves have been considered several times since World War II. The objections of the Fed to supplemental reserve requirements have centered on the undesirable effects of the proposals on central bank autonomy. Supplemental reserves "open the door" for the designation of other types of bank assets (mortgages or municipal bonds) as reserve-eligible. This use of reserve requirements on assets brings about the same type of political consequences as the broad bank supervisory authority described in Chapter 2. A host of powerful sectors would be expected to demand preferential reserve-eligible treatment by regulatory authorities. Similar exemptions from credit ceilings have created a highly politicized system of credit allocation in France (Goodman 1992).

Immediately after World War II, it appeared that the Fed would seek and implement supplemental reserve requirements on assets. The Board of Governors of the Federal Reserve System unanimously supported supplemental reserve requirements to encourage banks to acquire government securities. Marriner Eccles outlined a supplemental reserves proposal before the Committee on the Economic Report (the Taft Committee), but bank financial institutions uniformly opposed to the legislation. Other opponents to the supplemental reserves proposal included the President of the Federal Reserve Bank of New York, the Secretary of the Treasury and members of the Federal Advisory Council (Shay 1953). The proposal was outlined before several congressional committees and in the Annual Reports of the Board of Governors of the Federal Reserve System for 1945 and

1946, but failed to receive explicit endorsement by the Truman Administration in the annual Economic Report of the President.
During the Truman Administration, both the Board of Governors and the White House switched positions on the supplemental reserves question. After Marriner Eccles resigned from the Board of Governors January 1948 the CEA, ironically, became the primary advocate for supplemental reserves. The incoming Chairman of the Board of Governors, Thomas McCabe, did not prefer this type of change in the reserve requirement instrument but instead planned to use sweeping increases in existing reserve requirements to directly finance the massive purchase of long-term Treasury securities by the Fed.[24] In December 1948 (and again in 1952) the Truman Administration CEA proposed supplementary reserve requirements to induce commercial banks to hold government securities. The CEA advocated supplemental reserves in government securities for bank members of the Fed, as well as state banks in the Deposit Insurance System.[25] Responding to the 1952 proposals, William Martin, then Chairman of the Board of Governors, outlined his objections to Truman directly:

> The Board feels, as I do, that the specific recommendations by the Council for legislation to enact the so-called combination primary-security reserve plan at this time would be a gravely disturbing factor in the government bond market. It would be regarded by the financial community as a device to compel banks to buy government securities.
>
> Moreover, the experience of the last year with the discount and open market operations has served to illustrate the flexibility and effectiveness of the anti-inflationary use of these instruments.
>
> Our experience indicates that the same salutary results could not have been effected using the blunt and indiscriminate instrument of changes in reserve requirements which have seriously disruptive effects in the markets for government securities.[26]

The Truman proposals never received attention from Congress. Later proposals for similar reserve requirements were introduced in the Johnson White House and during the Carter administration. Treasury Department staff recommended supplementary reserve requirements to

Secretary of the Treasury Henry Fowler as a prospective component of the Johnson Administration economic stabilization program. Supplemental reserves in the from of Treasury securities and agency issues were advocated as a way to restrain the growth of credit in the economy and at the same time refund Treasury debt and sell agency securities.[27] In this case, the proposal never reached the Congress. Proposals for supplemental reserves were submitted from a prominent securities dealer to White House staff early in the Carter administration and then circulated among members of Congress. Fed staff outlined the drawbacks of the proposal in correspondence with Arthur Burns:

> A Treasury security reserve requirement sets a precedent for the use of credit market instruments for reserve purposes. This precedent might be used by Congress to pressure the Fed to support special interest assistance by extending the list of "reserve-eligible" assets to those such as mortgages, State and local bonds, and small business loans.[28]

Decision makers in the Fed perceived the new reserve requirements as potentially threatening to System autonomy. Support of particular sectors in the conduct of monetary policy seriously jeopardizes central bank autonomy. Fed decision makers oppose selective instruments such as supplemental reserves because of the incentives created for politicians interested in distribution of economic resources. These incentives are salient for members of Congress.

Reserve Requirements and the Composition of Bank Assets

Specific proposals by Congress to extend reserves to bank assets have been vigorously opposed by representatives of the Fed. In March 1971 and again in August 1974 members of Congress proposed to use reserve requirements to increase bank loans to home owners, small business, and municipal government. Legislation considered by the Senate in 1971 (S. 1201) specified that supplemental reserves should be used to direct credit toward home-building, state and local governments, small businesses, exporters, farms with sales of less than $100,000 a year, and areas of low income and high unemployment. Before receiving testimony on the bill, Committee Chairman William Proxmire argued that market forces do not allocate credit consistent with the public interest. He argued that "[t]he Fed must assume a greater degree of social responsibility or surrender its control over credit to another governmental institution."[29] The Senate bill generated considerable debate within the Fed and attracted coverage in the national media.[30]

Arthur Burns was compelled to offer a rebuttal to the charges from Congress that the central bank neglected the allocation of credit. Burns highlighted three undesirable consequences of the proposed legislation: First, System membership would be made even less attractive to banks. Second, reserve requirements that are tied to changing bank assets introduce uncertainty about future growth of loans and the money supply. Finally, the proposal subjects the Fed to "short run political pressures."[31] In the same hearing, the ABA complained that the legislation would "substitute arbitrary allocation of resources for market forces."[32]

Proposals for credit allocation were also considered in the House of Representatives in 1974. Before testimony was received on the bills, Arthur Burns expressed the vigorous opposition of the Board of Governors and the FOMC directly to Henry Reuss, Chairman of the House Banking and Currency Committee.[33] Andrew Brimmer, a Johnson appointee to the Board of Governors of the Federal Reserve System, also expressed his position on differential reserve requirements to Reuss. He specifically applauded congressional efforts to compel the Fed to allocate credit through the use of differential reserve requirements—what he described as a "common practice" among some foreign central banks to encourage banks to focus on "socially desirable lending."[34] Neither the 1971 Senate bill nor the 1974 House bill received a support from a majority of the members of Congress.

The Fed uses a variety of instruments to influence bank lending behavior and the allocation of credit, but none are either as overt or as rigid as reserve requirements on bank assets. Economic sectors adversely affected by monetary restraint may seek permanent statutory protection from credit restraint if direct and overt regulation is prescribed. During the early 1970s, the housing sector received special relief in the form of Regulation Q ceilings to protect thrift institutions from competition and direct support from a variety of other agencies that intervene in the market for mortgages. Opposition to reserve requirements on assets, from both within the Fed and from member financial institutions, was sufficient to block the explicit extension of protection of the housing sector to the reserve requirement instrument. Members of Congress did not aggressively pursue protection for the housing sector through updates to monetary policy instruments. Members of Congress instead relied on tax expenditures (the home mortgage interest tax deduction) and massive support for the home mortgage market through the development and subsidy of a secondary market for mortgages.[35] Neither mechanism (tax expenditures or the secondary market) requires explicit trade-offs across borrowers. If reserve requirements were imposed on banks assets, then the central bank would have to make decisions about the relative needs for credit across borrowers. Competing demands for reserve-eligibility would likely be resolved by regulators.

DISTRIBUTION OF RESERVES AND INCENTIVES FOR OVERSIGHT OF MONETARY POLICY

The reserve requirement instrument and the scope of required reserves have been the focus of reforms initiated by the banking committees in Congress, by the White House, and by the Board of Governors of the Federal Reserve System, as well as the topic of floor debate in the Congress. The Board of Governors of the Federal Reserve System implemented a variety of selective changes in the reserve requirement between 1948 and 1980. In many ways the development of reserve requirements resembles changes in the tax code. Requirements are increasingly complex. Highly specific policy targets and effects are achieved through the use of differential rates. There is a clear aversion to increasing the implicit tax burden. Distinct distributive effects underpin rule changes. It would appear that legislators have failed to act directly on the incentives created for them by the Fed. Members of Congress rarely exercised control over the specification of reserve requirements to affect acquisitions of funds (liability management) by banks. Members of Congress unsuccessfully sought control over the extension of the reserve requirements to bank assets—a direct attempt to influence bank lending behavior. The Board of Governors resisted these attempts to precisely allocate the burden of reserve requirements across financial institutions that support particular markets and borrowers (home buyers, small business, farmers). Rather than confront the central bank directly, members of Congress designed a battery of federal credit program to accomplish the same objective.

Members of Congress were able to deliver subsidized credit to the constituents the Fed resisted (agriculture, home buyers, small business). Decision makers in the Fed were able to preserve central bank autonomy. This trade-off between autonomy and capital allocation is further addressed in Chapter 7, below.

Decision makers in the Fed have unilaterally chosen to use reserve requirements to indirectly address distributive deficiencies in the markets for home mortgages and municipal securities. The reserve requirement instrument is appealing for this function. Between 1948 and 1980 commercial banks that submit to the costs of reserve requirements also benefit from discount window lending privileges and other System services: compliance with reserves requirements is accompanied by benefits. In addition, liability management incentives only indirectly allocate credit across member banks by affecting the relative prices of various sources of funds. There is no direct, overt regulation of credit end use embedded in the reserve requirement instrument.

Experience with other direct instruments indicates that a political process of credit allocation is not opposed by central bankers because of fears of market distortion, but instead because explicit allocation of credit would create incentives for Congress to closely supervise monetary policy.[36] Selective instruments such as differential reserve requirements clearly distort market mechanisms in the sense that bank choices about sources of funds are deliberately manipulated. The target of the selective intervention is limited: only member commercial banks are affected and the incentives for adjustment are modest. Broader reserve requirements upon assets more directly affect home buyers and builders, municipal government, small business, agriculture, and other credit-dependent sectors. The scope of potential political conflict is extraordinary. Reserve Bank presidents and members of the Board of Governors of the Federal Reserve System only rarely appeal to Congress for rule changes that can affect the distribution of reserve requirements across financial institutions and never introduce to Congress rule changes that could affect the distribution of monetary restraint across economic sectors. Members of the Board of Governors and Reserve Bank presidents retain discretion over the distribution of monetary restraint by proposing and adopting administrative rules that do not explicitly or systematically favor one particular economic sector over another. This strategy increases central bank autonomy over time.

NOTES

1. Letter with Enclosure. Chairman McCabe to Secretary Snyder. 4 Aug 1950. Folder: *Federal Reserve Banks—General.* Papers of John W. Snyder. Box #13. Dwight D. Eisenhower Library.

2. Letter. Arthur Burns to Senator Sparkman. 25 January 1974. Folder: *Reserve Requirements, 1974.* Box #B93. Papers of Arthur Burns. Gerald R. Ford Library.

3. Outline of Staff Presentation to the Board. 9 March 1973. Folder: *Monetary Policy—General.* Box #B80. Papers of Arthur Burns. Gerald R. Ford Library.

4. Memo. Office of General Counsel to John Snyder. 12 May 1949. Folder: *Federal Reserve Banks—General.* Box #13. Papers of John W. Snyder. Harry S Truman Library.

5. Memo. Sam Chase to Mr. Partee, Member, Board of Governors of the Federal Reserve System. 24 August 1973. Folder: *Reserve Requirements. January—August 1973.* Box # B93. Papers of Arthur Burns. Gerald R. Ford Library.

6. Letter. William Martin to John Sparkman, Chairman, Senate Committee on Banking and Currency. 1 March 1967. Folder: *Government. Federal Reserve Board: General: Federal Reserve, 1965-66 [1 of 2].* Papers of Henry Fowler. Box #26A. Lyndon Baines Johnson Library.

7. Letter. Arthur Burns to Senator Sparkman. 25 January 1974. Folder: *Reserve Requirements, 1974.* Box #B93. Papers of Arthur Burns. Gerald R. Ford Library.

8. Letter. Arthur Burns to Herbert Stein. 15 November 1972. Folder: *Reserve Requirements. June-December, 1972.* Box #B93. Papers of Arthur Burns. Gerald R. Ford Library.

9. Memo. Sam Chase to Mr. Partee. 24 August 1973. Folder: *Reserve Requirements. January-August, 1973.* Box #B93. Papers of Arthur Burns. Gerald R. Ford Library.

10. Policy Statement. Conference of State Bank Supervisors. 23 September 1973. Folder: *Reserve Requirements. September-October, 1973.* Box #B93. Papers of Arthur Burns. Gerald R. Ford Library

11. Memo. Reserve Requirements Policy Group to the Board of Governors. 28 Feb 1975. Folder: *Reserve Requirements—January-February, 1975.* Box #B94. Papers of Arthur Burns. Gerald R. Ford Library.

12. Letter. Division of Research and Statistics to the Board of Governors. Folder: *Reserve Requirements. (January 1972)* Box # B93. Federal Reserve Board Subject File. Papers of Arthur Burns. Gerald R. Ford Library.

13. *Congressional Quarterly.* Week ending July 3, 1959. Washington D.C.: Congressional Quarterly News Features.

14. Letter. Robert L. Cardon to Chairman Burns. 21 December 1971. Folder: *Reserve Requirements, 1971.* Box #B93. Papers of Arthur Burns. Gerald R. Ford Library.

15. Letter. Robert L. Cardon to Chairman Burns. 21 December 1971. Folder: *Reserve Requirements, 1971.* Box #B93. Papers of Arthur Burns. Gerald R. Ford Library.

16. Memo. Reserve Requirements Policy Group to the Board of Governors. 28 Feb 1975. Folder: Reserve Requirements. January-February 1975. Federal Reserve Board Subject File. Papers of Arthur Burns. Box #B94. Gerald R. Ford Library.

17. See *The Annual Report of the Board of Governors of the Federal Reserve System.* 1975. Washington D.C.: Board of Governors of the Federal Reserve System.

18. Memo. Division of Research and Statistics to the Board of Governors. 20 April 1970. Folder: *Reserve Requirements. (April-July 1970)* Box # B92. Federal Reserve Board Subject File. Papers of Arthur Burns. Gerald R. Ford Library.

19. Letter. A.W. Clausen, President of the Bank of America, to Arthur Burns. Folder: *Reserve Requirements. (September-December, 1970).* Box # B93. Federal Reserve Board Subject File. Papers of Arthur Burns. Gerald R. Ford Library.

20. Memo. Division of Research and Statistics to the Board of Governors. 11 June 1970. Folder: *Reserve Requirements, April-July 1970.* Box #B92. Federal Reserve Board Subject File. Arthur Burns Papers. Gerald R. Ford Library.

21. Federal Reserve Press Release. 17 August 1970. Folder: *Reserve Requirements. April-July, 1970.* Federal Reserve Board Subject File. Box #B92. Papers of Arthur Burns. Gerald R. Ford Library.

22. Memo. Division of Research and Statistics to the Board of Governors. 31 Aug 1973. Folder: *Reserve Requirements. January-August 1973.* Federal Reserve Board Subject File. Papers of Arthur Burns. Box #B93. Gerald R. Ford Library.

23. Memo. Office of the Managing Director for Research and Economic Policy to the Board of Governors. 18 Oct 1974. Folder: *Reserve Requirements, 1974.* Federal Reserve Board Subject File. Box # B93. Papers of Arthur Burns. Gerald R. Ford Library.

24. Statement of Thomas McCabe before the Senate Banking and Currency Committee. 29 July 1948. Folder: *OF 90 (1945-1947).* Official File. Papers of Harry S Truman. Harry S Truman Library.

25. Special Report to the President.—Anti-Inflation. 7 December 1948. Folder: *Special Report to the President—Anti-Inflation.* Papers of Leon Keyserling. Harry S Truman Library.

26. Letter. William Martin to President Truman. 8 Feb 1952. Folder: *Special Report to The President—Monetary Policy and Reserve Requirements, February 7, 1952.* Box #3. Papers of Leon Keyserling. Harry S Truman Library.

27. Memo. Fred Deming to Henry Fowler. 23 June 1966. Folder: *Domestic Economy: Monetary Policy, General: 1966.* Box #17D. Papers of Henry Fowler. Lyndon Baines Johnson Library.

28. Memo. Edward Ettin, Division of Research and Statistics, to Arthur Burns. 4 Jul 1977. Folder: *Reserve Requirements. March 1975—December 1977.* Federal Reserve Board Subject File. Box #B93. Papers of Arthur Burns. Gerald R. Ford Library.

29. Opening Statement. William Proxmire. 31 March 1971. Before the Subcommittee on Financial Institutions. Senate Banking and Currency Committee. Folder: *Proxmire bill (S.1201) March 1971 (3).* Box #B90. Papers of Arthur Burns. Gerald R. Ford Library.

30. "Fed As Allocator" *New York Times.* 28 March 1968 (F4)

31. Statement. Arthur Burns. 31 March 1971. Before the Subcommittee on Financial Institutions. Senate Banking and Currency Committee. Folder: *Proxmire bill (S.1201) March 1971 (3).* Box #B90. Papers of Arthur Burns. Gerald R. Ford Library.

32. Letter. Clifford Somer, ABA, to Senator Proxmire. 1 April 1971. Folder: *Proxmire Bill (S.1201). March 1971. (3).* Box #B90. Papers of Arthur Burns. Gerald R. Ford Library.

33. Letter. Arthur Burns to Henry Reuss. 29 July 1974. Folder: *Reuss, Henry. January 1972—January 1975. Congressional Correspondence.* Box #O16. Papers of Arthur Burns. Gerald R. Ford Library.

34. Letter. Andrew Brimmer to Henry Reuss. 5 Aug 1974. Folder: *Reuss, Henry. January 1972—January 1975. Congressional Correspondence.* Box #O16. Papers of Arthur Burns. Gerald R. Ford Library.

35. See Chapter 7 for discussion of federal support for the mortgage market.

36. See Chapter 5 for a discussion of postwar experience with direct selective controls.

CHAPTER 4

Open Market Transactions: The Scope and Frequency of Capital Market Intervention

Fairly specific rules define the type of daily market transactions that the central bank uses to implement monetary policy. These rules are revised for ostensibly technical reasons on an infrequent basis. The changing rules are important constraints on social actors with a stake in monetary policy outcomes. The rules have distinct political consequences which are evident to members of Congress, economists, White House staff, and the members of the FOMC. Central bankers may limit the types of market transactions undertaken in order to impose their own policy goals upon both office holders and agencies that carry and refund outstanding debt, including the Treasury. Central bankers may also choose to broaden market transactions in order to meet specific objectives of elected officials. Changes in the rules governing open market transactions have alternately diminished and expanded the options of elected officials confronted with monetary and economic problems. One goal of FOMC updates to open market procedures is to escape specific statutory direction of open market activity. Decision makers in the Fed have been reluctant to consistently support particular economic sectors through the purchase of particular types of securities. Consistent with decisions to reject selective credit controls and resist reserve requirements on bank assets, members of the Board of Governors and the FOMC are reluctant to use direct purchases of government securities to affect costs of credit and capital for particular classes of borrowers. One exception to this fairly narrow use of open market transactions is experimentation with purchase of debt issued by the Federal National Mortgage Association (FNMA) in the 1970s.

Overall, the variation in open market practice after World War II is remarkable. The postwar period includes the strict subordination of open market activity to debt management objectives immediately after the war, the highly restrictive Bills Only rules adopted after 1953, the liberalization of open market activity in the 1960s and 1970s, and a return to narrow operating practices after 1981. Each set of changes in operating procedure redistributed the burdens of monetary adjustment from some sectors of the economy to others and compelled other government agencies and social actors to update expectations about central bank behavior. The routine purchase of government securities by the central bank remains the fundamental instrument of monetary policy.

CENTRAL BANK TRANSACTIONS IN GOVERNMENT SECURITIES

Central banks and public debt

The relationship between monetary policy choices and government debt has its origins in the earliest attempts to establish reliable and routine access to credit for the state. Smith (1990) describes the first experiences of national banks as "a series of exchanges between the needy government and an accommodating corporation." A private bank was typically given special and profitable authority to issue bank notes (currency) in exchange for quite generous lending terms for the national treasury. Gradually, the function of note issue and the management of public debt have come under direct control of the state. Proponents of "free banking" and public choice critics of central banking claim that the monopoly on note issue creates irresistible inflationary temptations for elected officials (Brennan and Buchanan 1981). The central bank now typically carries out both the introduction and regulation of currency and the maintenance of an orderly market for public debt.

The Fed actively supports and monitors the regular refunding and issue of debt by the Treasury. Day-to-day purchases of government securities to carry out monetary policy objectives in this context are *open market operations*. Purchases and sales of short-term securities are used to meet a target *federal funds rate*—the interest rate charged on overnight interbank loans used by commercial banks to meet reserve requirements. The federal funds market responds to trading activities of the Federal Reserve Bank of New York carried out under the authority of the FOMC. Daily trading activity is carried out by traders at the Federal Reserve Bank of New York, typically in consultation with a member of the Board of Governors (Havrilesky 1993). The federal funds rate target is updated every seven to eight weeks at regular meetings of the FOMC.

The federal funds market is a principal source of cash used by banks to meet reserve requirements, so the funds rate manipulated by the Fed is directly related to the rates of interest on other short-term money market instruments—especially the Treasury bill.[1] This link ensures that the open market transactions of the Federal Reserve Bank of New York affect the price of money for nonbank financial intermediaries, as well as commercial banks. Movements in interest rates produced by open market activity attract the attention of holders of a variety of forms of wealth. As a consequence, the purchase and sale of government securities by the Fed is perhaps the most highly scrutinized activity of any government agency. Securities dealers, stock brokers and institutional investors analyze interest rate movements and FOMC decisions in order to forecast and anticipate System activity and trade affected securities profitably.

The Market for Government Debt in the United States

Since the end of the Civil War the government securities market has principally been an over-the-counter market dominated by a few specialized dealer firms. The market was broadened considerably during World War I from a narrow base of commercial banks to include nonbank and individual investors as well as government agents (principally, the War Finance Corporation). The Department of the Treasury handled most of its securities transactions during the interwar years through the New York Stock Exchange. After 1925, Treasury transactions were handled in an over-the-counter dealer market that has been regulated, supported, and supervised by the Fed.[2] The Fed currently holds about 10 percent of all outstanding federal public debt, from a low of less than 5 percent of all federal public debt in 1950 and a peak of 15 percent of all federal public debt in 1977 (Economic Report of the President, Various Years).

The United States engaged in a massive debt financing campaign during World War II with an important purchasing role and market clearing function for the Fed. Fed purchases during the war maintained the prices of government bonds at or above original auction levels. Stable bond prices encouraged owners of public debt (commercial banks and nonbank investors) to hold and acquire debt, rather than sell outstanding issues. Pegging, the practice of maintaining specific yields on government securities, was perceived as a wartime financing necessity. The day-to-day purchase of Treasury securities for the purposes of conducting monetary policy (and affecting macroeconomic outcomes) was subordinated to the need for stability in the government securities market. During this period, the open market activities of the Federal Reserve Bank of New York were directly coordinated with the Secretary of the Treasury and his staff.[3]

Explaining Changes in Open Market Transaction Rules

The FOMC has changed several rules related to open market operations since the end of World War II. The most important changes specify the types of government securities bought and sold in open market operations. Important changes occurred in August 1950, March 1951, March 1953, April 1955, February 1961, and December 1969. The timing of two of the more significant rule changes (in early 1961 and early 1953) suggests a simple political explanation for changes in monetary policy instruments. Important changes occur on or near presidential inaugurations when a new party controls the White House. The simple explanation is not compelling. Some rule changes benefit the new president, other changes are opposed by the new president. The implications of the each of the rule changes for White House options and policy are described below.

Three sets of rule changes have particularly important consequences for the transformation of the Fed: the Treasury Accord (1951), the adoption of the Bills Only doctrine (1953), and the extension of open market transactions to long-term securities and agency issues (1961 and 1969). Each innovation in open market procedure was controversial and each innovation was introduced as a modest technical adjustment to changing economic and capital market conditions. These changes in open market practices ultimately affect the strategies, preferences, and actions of elected officials. Rule changes are intentionally undertaken to minimize Fed involvement in conflict over the distribution of monetary restraint. The rule changes reduce the chance that members of Congress or the White House will use the central bank to implement permanent statutory protection of particular segments of money and capital markets including the bond market and the market for home mortgages. The rule changes, in each instance, increase central bank autonomy. In two of the three cases, congressional action is neither required for the Fed to act nor is there any congressional response to undo the rule changes.

THE FEDERAL RESERVE-TREASURY ACCORD

Debt Management and the Truman White House

During World War II, close administrative coordination of Treasury debt sales and Fed open market operations was intended to maintain stable and orderly markets for government securities. In practice, informal coordination of open market activities between the Treasury and the Fed maintained bond prices and yields at particular levels.[4] This administrative arrangement persisted from November 1941 through April 1947. The FOMC allowed yields on short-term issues to rise above wartime ceilings in 1948 and yields on long-term issues were allowed to rise to wartime ceilings after 1950.

A March 1951 accord between the Department of the Treasury and the Fed officially discontinued Fed wartime policies of supporting any Treasury issues at specific yields in the money markets. The 1951 accord was perceived by members of the CEA as a direct repudiation of the preferences of the White House. A majority of the CEA advocated direct regulation of commercial bank lending and open market operations to stabilize yields on government securities at pre-accord levels.[5]

In his 1948 Economic Report to the Congress, President Truman explicitly committed his administration to maintaining the market value of nearly 250 billion dollars in outstanding Treasury bonds:[6]

> The financial world should rest easy that the investment market will not be subject to the demoralization which swept over it in 1920 when the unsupported market for Government bonds fell about 20 percent below par. *Economic Report of the President for 1948*

The CEA under President Truman was an early opponent of upwardly flexible interest rates, preferring instead to selectively restrain expanding credit for real estate transactions and consumer credit purchases to prevent inflation.[7] The White House also advocated increased reserve requirements to address the problem of credit and monetary inflation. Truman specifically and unambiguously directed the Chairman of the Board of Governors of the Federal Reserve System to continue open market operations in government bonds to maintain bond prices at par.[8] The potential for conflict between the administration and the Fed was the subject of consultations between Truman and his CEA. John D. Clark, a member of the CEA, outlined the problem for Truman:

> The relation of monetary policies to national prosperity and the problem of managing the huge national debt forbid a division of authority which permits the directors of the central bank to adopt policies which are inconsistent with those of the Administration elected by the people. Nor is it tolerable to compel the officers of the Administration to resort to persuasion and blandishment in order to secure complete cooperation by central bank authorities in positive support of the administration program.[9]

The Retreat from Pegging

Before 1950 the Fed purchased Treasury issues in the open market to maintain prices and yields of government securities consistent with White House objectives. Banks could exploit this constraint upon the Fed by selling government securities at face value and then using the capital to make loans to consumers and firms. Any Fed action to reduce the growth of money and credit aggregates through increased reserve requirements or discount window borrowing restrictions was futile given the volume of securities that banks could sell to meet reserve requirements without borrowing from the Federal Reserve Banks. Commercial banks sold 5.8 billion dollars in government securities in 1947, 6.3 billion in 1948, and 5 billion in 1950 (Economic Report of the President, 1950).

Fed credit policy after 1950 drove interest rates on short-term government securities above wartime ceilings. The increase in bill yields was principally designed to compel commercial banks to borrow from Federal Reserve Banks rather than liquidate bill holdings to meet reserve deficiencies.[10] Treasury staff perceived the increase in bill yields as a setback for financing strategies:

> The Federal Reserve sold the idea that it had to purchase short-term issues in order to support Treasury refunding operations. Actually, Treasury refunding operations would not have needed support, had it not been for the adverse Federal Reserve open-market operations and the continued rumors that the Federal Reserve was going to force higher rates.[11]

The eventual result of climbing yields on both short-term and long-term securities was an Oval Office confrontation between Truman and the entire FOMC in 1951. Truman mistakenly believed he extracted from the Committee an explicit promise to maintain bond prices at current levels while the administration studied the problems of debt management and credit policy.

Provisions and Consequences of the 1951 Accord

Before the CEA or other White House staff could develop an alternative to the flexible monetary policy implemented in early 1951, the Fed negotiated an agreement with the Treasury under which the price on long-term bonds would be supported at just below par until the end of the Truman Administration. A majority of the CEA considered the compromise a severe blow to the debt management program of the administration.[12]

The Federal Reserve—Treasury Accord was an unambiguous repudiation of the preferences of the CEA and a retreat from the Truman Administration commitment to stable bond prices in 1948. Most scholarly work on the politics of monetary policy does not discuss this period of overt conflict and instead examines more congenial interactions after the Accord was implemented. Under the provisions of the Accord, central bankers in the Fed publicly undercut White House objectives in a critical period. Directed to explicitly support a particular segment of the money and capital markets, the bond market, members of the FOMC chose to reject executive political influence. Members of Congress, although active in investigating the actions of the Board of Governors, never intervened to either discipline the Fed or reinforce administration objectives. Members of Congress tolerated, and implicitly encouraged, central bank autonomy. A return to pegging, or other administrative arrangements that placed the Fed under the influence of the executive, was never advocated by members of Congress.

After the Accord, the FOMC has been more careful to signal the limitations of central bank compliance with executive demands before overt conflict becomes inevitable. Despite this signaling, the controversy over executive discretion and open market activities did not end with the Treasury Accord. Important changes in operating procedures since the Treasury Accord have narrowed and then expanded the scope of White House influence over open market activity. The changes are the best examples of how institutional rules, in the form of central bank operating procedures, can frustrate elected officials.

THE BILLS ONLY DOCTRINE

Immediately after the inauguration of Dwight Eisenhower and the termination of the provisions of the 1951 Accord, the FOMC began operating under a narrow set of rules for transactions in government securities: Bills Only. The Bills Only doctrine governed Fed open market operations throughout the Eisenhower Administration. New and broader operating procedures were approved in conjunction with Fed participation in Operation Twist, a 1961 Kennedy Administration program to lower the balance of payments deficit, and again in 1966 when Congress authorized open market transactions in government securities issued by the various federal agencies.

Bills Only practices confined open market purchases to short-term government securities (Treasury bills). This operating policy foreclosed all but exceptional open market operations to support the market for Treasury bonds. Sale and purchase of Treasury bonds were a negligible component of net open market transactions after 1950. The annual net purchases of bonds by the Fed are displayed in Figure 4. Open market purchases of Treasury bonds effectively ceased during the Eisenhower Administration. This is an anomaly. Bond purchases were an important component of open market activity during the Truman administration and continued well after the termination of the Kennedy Administration balance of payments initiative in the early 1960s.

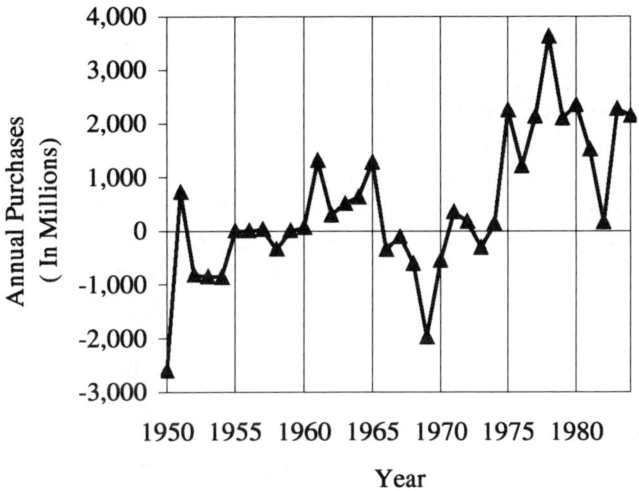

Figure 4
Net open market purchases of Treasury bonds (1950-1985).

Source: Anuual Report of the Board of Governors of the Federal Reserve System, Various Years.

Adoption of the restrictive rules

An FOMC directive approved in March 1953 announced the intention of the FOMC to limit the purchases of government securities to Treasury issues with a maturity not exceeding one year. The language of the directive was revised in September and December of 1953 to make the policy change appear as a permanent and fixed rule for open market transactions. The new language was highly controversial. Two FOMC members dissented from the September 1953 FOMC directive. Allan Sproul, the President of the Federal Reserve Bank of New York, and O.S. Powell, a Reserve Bank president, opposed the policy change. The FOMC dissents were not trivial acts. The dissents reflected internal conflict within the Fed over the retreat from flexible monetary policy as implemented in 1951. Robert Roosa (at the Federal Reserve Bank of New York during the Bills Only period and, later,

Undersecretary of the Treasury for Monetary Affairs) notes that one dimension of the conflict was tension between Board of Governors staff and the Reserve Bank Presidents. The Board planned to centralize narrow Fed authority in Washington D.C.; decision makers in the Reserve Banks advocated a more decentralized and activist approach to monetary policy.[13]

Throughout the Bills Only period the most vigorous proponents of flexible operating procedures were within the Federal Reserve Bank of New York. Allan Sproul, President of the Federal Reserve Bank of New York until 1956, argued that transactions in bills only were disingenuous, an attempt to disguise the "essential linkages between such actions and the cost and availability of credit" (Ritter 1980). Sproul also claimed the doctrine was a handicap to monetary authorities. He was suspicious of "policy norms" that could guide central bank decisions in the open market as a substitute for discretion and flexible procedure. He was openly critical of the advocates of Bills Only, "hell bent to publish the rules of the game" at the expense of monetary policy flexibility (Ritter 1980).

Carson (1966) suggested that the Bills Only controversy was one component of a broader conflict between academic economists and central bank decision makers—a conflict over how central bank activity should be directed at economic stabilization over the business cycle. Monetary economists suggested that more aggressive central bank activity was desirable and practical. Practitioners among the Board of Governors resisted the broader central bank role and favored a more narrow definition of central bank functions. Ironically, less than twenty years later, monetary economists—notably Milton Friedman and his associates—would advocate statutory rules that specified the growth rate of the money supply and eliminated central bank discretion altogether.

Executive Influence and Bills Only rules

It is tempting to conclude that the initiation of Bill Only in March 1953 simply reflected the preferences of the new Republican administration. The Chairman of the Board of Governors of the Federal Reserve System introduced the Bills Only operating practices as part of a "Transition to Free Markets" consistent with other administration economic policies.[14] The introduction was misleading. There were no proponents of Bills Only practices in either the CEA or among other White House staff. Eisenhower and his CEA advocated broad securities purchases by the Fed to correct the selective effects of monetary restraint. Many in the Eisenhower Administration believed the Fed should act to directly bring down the long-term interest rates that affect the markets for municipal bond issues, home mortgages, and government securities.

Arthur Burns, Chairman of the CEA under Eisenhower, became increasingly frustrated with unwillingness of economists in the Fed to recognize and remedy the disproportionate effects of monetary and credit restraint on credit-dependent sectors such as the construction industry, state and local government, and small business. In the fall of 1956 Burns described the problem:

> The fellows at the Board live in an ivory tower. I have tried to make them see the point that a policy of credit restraint has certain unintended effects, particularly with respect to small business, and that it is only proper that we do what we can to mitigate these side effects.[15]

Other members of the Council concurred:

> The plain fact is that monetary measures to restrain nonmonetary upward price pressures has a perverse selectivity which it would be euphemistic to call simply the impersonal forces of the free market in operation.[16]

Speaking to the Cabinet in late 1956, Arthur Burns advocated direct action by the Board of Governors to address these disparities.[17] Other White House staff suggested that congressional remedies were necessary and desirable.[18] By rejecting external appeals to change internal rules, decision makers in the Fed were compelling the White House and the Congress to consider ways to allocate or distribute credit that did not implicate the Fed in the distributive choices. The White House was ultimately dependent on members of Congress to create remedies for economic sectors affected by the monetary policy choices of the Fed. The Congress responded by initiating a broad range of federal credit programs to ensure the orderly flow of funds to a number of economic sectors, notably the mortgage market and small business.

As the Bills Only rules persisted, CEA staff became increasingly skeptical of the effectiveness of Fed strategy. The White House was particularly frustrated when commercial bank holdings of government securities reached postwar lows during 1956:

> Thus commercial banks, by circumventing the Fed, may in a sense be throwing off the pressure of contraction on other sectors of the economy.
>
> I suspect that present Fed policy has been hampered by adherence to the "Bills Only" doctrine. Banks hold relatively few bills.
>
> Experience with monetary policy during the last year has shown that its operation is more subtle and complex and its effects much more difficult to assess than either opponents or proponents of monetary policy have generally conceded.[19]

As late as 1957, the Eisenhower CEA recommended that the FOMC abandon the Bills Only doctrine in order to address rising interest rates in long-term markets.[20]

PERSISTENCE OF BILLS ONLY

Despite repeated demands from the White House and internal pressure from the Federal Reserve Bank of New York, the FOMC restricted open market activity to Treasury bills throughout the 1950s. The primary justification for Bills Only (the so-called Riefler doctrine) was that limiting System purchases to Treasury bills reduced uncertainty among securities dealers about the extent of future System activity in the securities market. Stable expectations encouraged the growth and broadening of the securities market.[21] One important and controversial component of the Riefler doctrine was the claim that long-term bond rates, more than rates in other markets, are particularly vulnerable to speculation and volatility. Staff at the Board of Governors defended the Bills Only doctrine on these grounds in responses to congressional monetary policy inquiries (the Flanders Committee) in 1954.[22] Support for long-term securities was therefore confined to exceptional periods of market disorder. The Fed was compelled to support the bond market under these extraordinary conditions for a brief five-day period in July of 1958. This surprising market disorder under Bills Only prompted a

Treasury-Federal Reserve Study of the Government Securities Market (July 1959). Defending Bills Only, the study placed primary blame for poor market performance on persistent budget deficits and competition for funds from federal agency issues and obligations.

Observers of monetary policy during the 1950s discounted the claims of Fed decision makers about Bills Only and specifically challenged Fed conclusions about dealer expectations and the performance of the bond market. Contemporary observers identified two other motivations for the choices of the Board of Governors and the Open Market Committee. First, it was argued that Bills Only practices were preferable for central bank decision makers because short-term purchases only indirectly influence the behavior of market interest rates (Carson 1966). Second, it was anticipated that Bills Only could compel responsible debt management at the Treasury (Degen 1987, Timberlake 1965).

Indirect Effects

Bills Only practices rely on the government securities market for the indirect transmission of monetary policy to nonbank financial intermediaries and individual borrowers. Since the end of World War II, the market for government securities has expanded to include a wide variety of investors and intermediaries. Commercial bank ownership of public debt has fallen, while nonbank investor ownership (especially ownership by international investors) has increased. Figure 5 reveals the magnitude of the changes in ownership.

Decision makers in the Fed rely on the broad securities market to indirectly transmit the effects of monetary restraint to borrowers in a variety of markets. The direct effects of open market activity—increases in the federal funds rate—create incentives for commercial banks and other nonbank financial institutions to adjust the composition of their portfolios. Depending on the degree of segmentation in capital markets, adjustments to changes in the yields of short term debt instruments affects interest rates in a variety of markets.[23] By manipulating the federal funds rate, the Fed can indirectly affect outcomes in long-term markets.

Carson (1966) observed that unlike other more direct monetary control strategies, the Bills Only approach mitigates the role that the Fed plays in determining the level and term structure of interest rates.

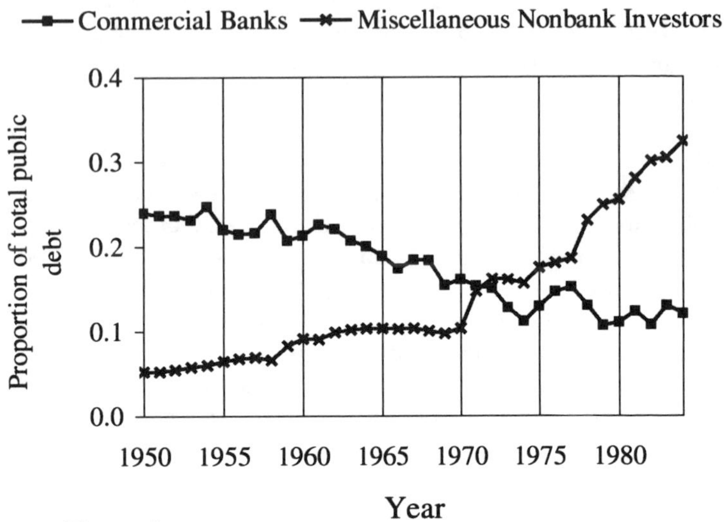

Figure 5
Commercial and miscellaneous nonbank ownership of publc debt (1950-1985).

Source: Economic Report of the President, Various Years.

Since the Fed did not operate directly in the market for long-term securities, prices and yields in these markets must be a function of private demands and preferences, not FOMC action or choices. Demands for lower interest rates from borrowers in the long-term markets could simply not be accommodated by Fed decision makers under Bills Only practices. Carson explains the political appeal of the restrictive rules:

> Given [responsibilities] to Congress, and the need to serve the national interest, the Federal Reserve is forced to explain its sometimes politically distasteful policies in ways that will minimize political hostilities. This is done, if our interpretation is correct, by de-emphasizing the role that the Federal Reserve plays in determining the level and structure of interest rates and by adopting operating techniques which, while somewhat arbitrary, give the appearance of impersonality and are, in fact, less arbitrary than some available alternatives.

> This image of the Board's powers is certainly more acceptable to the general public than that of a monolithic monetary authority; unfortunately, the desire to project it may lead the central bank to adopt attitudes and techniques that interfere with its own—as well as the public's—ultimate goals (Carson 1966, 314).

Others argue that a similar political logic motivated the rejection of selective credit controls in the 1950s and the temporary shift from narrow interest rates targets to rigid monetary aggregate targets in 1979 (Ahearn 1963, Lombra 1988). In each case, substantial political opposition was expected to accompany the ultimate effects of System operations. Credit controls were expected to generate opposition from consumers and lenders. Money aggregate targets were expected to generate historically high nominal interest rtes. By confining System activity to narrow open market activity or (in 1979) by attributing interest rate increases to market adjustments, Fed decision makers could deny direct responsibility for politically unpopular outcomes. Lombra (1988) reports that senior Fed decision makers valued the "political sheltering" that rigid money aggregate targets could provide (Lombra 1988, 347).

Like the later targeting experience, Bills Only afforded the Fed shelter from growing demands for lower interest rates from the home building industry, small business, and municipal government. The Fed adopted Bills Only in a critical period of nascent central bank autonomy. Bills Only was introduced immediately after the expiration of the formal terms of the Treasury Accord and U.S. experience with an autonomous central bank was limited. Fed resistance to executive demands for more active intervention was not met by a vigorous congressional response. Congress would not be expected to advocate a change in operating procedure that required more coordination and consultation between an executive office (the Treasury) and the Fed.

Debt Management

Debt management and monetary policy goals remained wedded even after the formal decoupling of debt management from open market activity under the terms of the Treasury Accord. In the early part of the Eisenhower Administration, the Treasury made a number of attempts to tailor debt management to Bills Only practices. Debt management policy within the Department of the Treasury in the first Eisenhower Administration centered on how best to finance public debt in the short-term markets continuously supported by the Fed. Neil Jacoby, a member of the CEA, described federal debt management strategy to White House Economic Councilor Gabriel Hauge:

> Since mid-1953 the Treasury Department has followed the policy of financing governmental needs for funds by the issuance of short-term obligations, thereby avoiding competition with business corporations, municipalities, builders, and other users of long-term funds in order to keep long-term rates down.[24]

Both the CEA and the Undersecretary of the Treasury for Monetary Affairs advocated short-term debt financing in order to preserve capital for long-term investment in private markets.[25] Other anticipated benefits included lower debt service costs.[26] Fed decisions about open market rules affected these policy choices in the executive branch

The short-term financing arrangements advocated by economists in the CEA were not uncontroversial. Proponents of long-term debt financing argued that a modest rate premium could substantially lower uncertainty about future interest costs. The penalty (competition with other users of long-term credit—such as home buyers and municipalities) was perceived as acceptable. In the second Eisenhower Administration, the CEA remained advocates of short-term financing, but the Undersecretary for Monetary Affairs (with White House approval) publicly advocated long-term debt financing and higher long-term interest rates to attract private funds to the capital markets.[27]

Members of Congress played an important role in the resolution of this conflict. Congressional reluctance to raise interest rates on federal securities maturing in more than five years (a 1918 ceiling of 4.25%) conspired to prevent the proponents of long-term financing from experimenting with issues in the long end of the market. Interest rates could not rise above the ceilings set by Congress, so neither Fed action nor Treasury demands could bring about the desired changes in the market for long-term government debt. Congress authorized an increase in the interest rate ceilings on Series E and H savings bonds in September of 1959, but refused to eliminate the 4.25% ceiling on long bonds until much later.

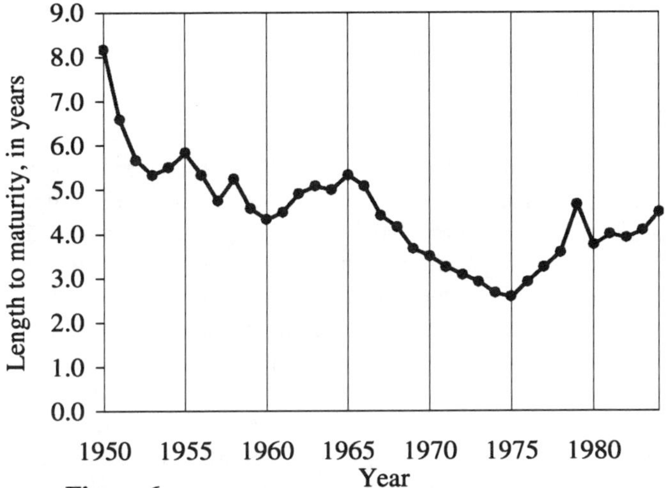

Figure 6
Average length to maturity of marketable public debt (1950-1985).

Source: Economic Report of the President, Various Years.

One result of the short-term financing strategy was that the average length to maturity of the public debt reached record low levels during the Eisenhower Administration. Figure 6 displays the length to maturity of marketable public debt from 1950 to 1985. In 1959 Treasury staff calculated that 40% of all marketable debt would require refinancing in the following calendar year. The fear of most market observers was that these heavy refinancing demands would force short-term interest rates to new postwar highs.[28] Direct action by Congress or the White House to meet these concerns over rising interest rates was never required. Ultimately, a series of rule changes in the Fed would simultaneously address emerging international balance of payments problems and the domestic debt financing problems. Despite the new and broader operating procedures, the length to maturity of the public debt continued to decline and eventually dropped well below the 1959 threshold. The propensity to finance debt in the short end of the market was only briefly reversed during the 1960s when the Fed began to actively purchase long-term bonds and in the late 1970s when bond purchases increased dramatically under Arthur Burns.

AMENDING THE RULES

Despite the persistent defense of Bills Only practices during the Eisenhower Administration, the FOMC made a series of changes in operating procedure in the 1960s. The changes first expanded the scope of open market operations to debt instruments not issued by the government, then to long-term government securities, and finally to securities issued by government agencies other than the Treasury. The transition from Bills Only to broader central bank intervention in capital markets was neither a sudden (punctuated) innovation nor a capitulation to executive influence. Vigorous congressional oversight also fails to explain the timing of the FOMC actions, although statutory changes were required to permit Fed purchases of securities issued by government agencies other than the Treasury.

Bankers' Acceptances (1955)

Prior to changes to rules affecting government securities, the FOMC expanded the scope of open market operations to include bankers' acceptances. Bankers' acceptances are short-term instruments used to finance international transactions. Typically, acceptances substitute for a direct loan to finance inventories used for export or for a loan to provide payment for imports. In March 1955 the Fed began to enter into repurchase agreements (a short-term open market acquisition) for bankers' acceptances. Decision makers at the Fed considered ending transactions in the acceptance market as early as 1970, but purchase and sale of bankers' acceptances persisted until 1984.[29]

The explicit purpose of supporting the growing acceptance market was to "facilitate smooth short run adjustments of balance of payments" by encouraging bank and dealer trade and warehousing of acceptances (Federal Reserve Bulletin, March 1955). Open market purchases of bankers' acceptances was a notable innovation in central bank practice. The new rules demonstrated that open market transactions could be used to facilitate particular types of financial intermediation. Open market purchases could be used to make a particular type of debt instrument attractive and encourage particular types of economic transactions (in this case, trade). Selective and discretionary purchase and sale of other debt instruments (notably, the issues of federal agencies) could then presumably be used to implement a broader regime of credit allocation by the central bank. In an effort to remedy a fairly narrow and discrete problem in financial markets, a weak acceptance market and persistent balance of payments deficits, decision makers in the Fed demonstrated how open market activities could abet the allocation of credit and capital across financial markets.

Government Bonds (1961)

Open market operations were officially extended to long-term government securities in 1961. A Task Force Report released by President-elect Kennedy specifically advocated Fed purchases of longer-term securities.[30] Libby (1987) argues that this pressure from the Kennedy Administration—and the persistent resistance from the Federal Reserve Bank of New York to Bills Only practices—precipitated the rule change. Ahearn (1963) concluded that the repudiation of Bills Only was an admission of the technical failure of Bills Only manifested in the growing balance of payments deficit. The rule change was a response to an objective economic outcome that was undesirable and (potentially) remediable: the balance of payments deficit.

Open market operations in long-term issues were part of broader Kennedy Administration program designated "Operation Twist." The program was designed to address the balance of payments deficit by allowing short-term interest rates to climb and at the same time maintaining low long-term interest rates to stimulate domestic economic growth. Heavy Treasury demands for short-term funds were to nudge short rates up, while open market purchases of bonds were to bring long rates down. Many bankers believed purchasing activity by the Fed in the long end of the securities market was tantamount to a return to explicit pegging of interest rates (representative is Beckhart 1972). The Kennedy program was not successful as a solution to the balance of payments problem, but purchases of long-term securities by the Fed have persisted since 1960.

Rule changes that extended open market activity to long-term securities signaled a closer relationship between the White House and the Fed. Open market operations could be used to facilitate a particular administration objective and bring about outcomes that were consistent with other administration policy goals. Disagreement within the Fed made it more likely that administration demands would be satisfied, but the 1961 rule change demonstrated the utility of change in central bank procedure for affecting money and capital market outcomes. The lesson did not escape members of Congress.

Federal agency obligations (1966)

In 1966 Congress granted the Fed narrow statutory authority to purchase securities issued by federal agencies other than the Treasury, such as the Federal National Mortgage Association and the Federal Home Loan Bank Board. Optimistic about the application of the 1966 authority, Lyndon Johnson hoped to induce the Fed to massively support the mortgage market by purchasing issues of the Federal Home Loan Bank Board. Despite an explicit request from Johnson, Gardner Ackley, Chairman of the CEA, refused to pressure the Board of Governors to make such purchases.[31] The Open Market Desk purchased a modest amount of agency issues on the open market in the second quarter of 1967, but active trading in agency issues did not occur until the appointment of Arthur Burns as Chairman of the Board of Governors of the Federal Reserve System.

Congress considered a broader agency issue authorization in 1968, but the proposal was defeated by a single vote in the Senate. William Martin described the prospective changes in rules governing non-Treasury issues as a "prostitution of agency" (New York Times, 07/25/68). Mayer (1982) reports that the Board of Governors specifically resisted open market operations in agency issues to avoid the kind of political intervention contemplated by the Johnson White House. The position of the Board of Governors was outlined for incoming Chairman Arthur Burns in 1970:

> The political argument against even small-scale operations in agency issues (which I believe was held by Chairman Martin, though, of course, not emphasized publicly, as well as by some other members of the Board and the FOMC) is that this would represent a foot in the door for the various agencies and would then expose the System to undesirable political pressures from individual agencies to help support their own operations.[32]

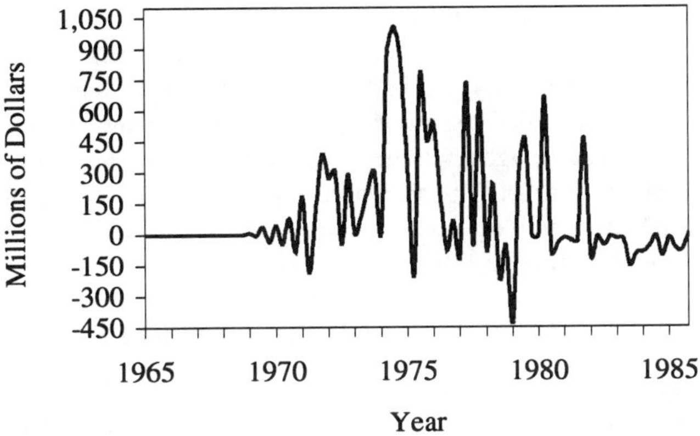

Figure 7
Net open market purchases of federal agency issues (1965-1985).

Source: Flow of Funds Coded Tables.
Board of Governors of the Federal Reserve System.
See notes for additional information.

The argument must have been unpersuasive for Burns. The Fed actively purchased agency issues in the open market after 1970. Figure 7 displays open market activity in agency issues after the rule change. There was virtually no open market activity in agency issues prior to the appointment of Burns as Chairman and no net purchases of agency issues after 1981. The purchases of agency issues in the early 1970s were, in practice, primarily transactions in the issues of the Federal National Mortgage Association (FNMA).[33] The intent was to channel funds into the mortgage market by encouraging the growth of a nascent secondary mortgage market. The real amount of the transactions was remarkably high and at times inconsistent with aggregate open market transactions. In the third quarter of 1974 the Fed purchased nearly 1 billion dollars worth of agency issues while at the same time selling nearly 125 million dollars of conventional Treasury securities.[34]

The series of rule changes undertaken with the aid of Congress after 1960 appear to be specific attempts to tailor the rules of open market transactions to small and discrete financial market problems. Initial open market activities in bankers' acceptances and long term securities were intended to slow the growth of the balance of payments deficit. Purchases of agency issues were intended to remedy problems in the mortgage market. The adoption of broader transactions rules led the FOMC to selectively use specific types of transactions to meet specific credit market objectives.

IMPACT OF CONGRESS UNDER THE NEW RULES

The variety of debt instruments that are the targets of open market operations—bankers' acceptances, Treasury bills, agency issues, and Treasury bonds—suggests that particular social objectives, such as lower home mortgage interest rates, lower public debt service, or broader international trade may be achieved using monetary policy instruments. Choices of practices and rules for central bank transactions in government securities are relatively clear indicators of how central bankers will support these various goals. Disputes over whether or not sets of transactions should be excluded (by adopting new rules) can be interpreted as a dispute over whether or not the Fed should attempt to remedy specific problems. A strategic central banker can therefore use rules to foreclose or limit the application of preferential treatment to particular sectors of the economy. It would not be unreasonable to expect that the composition of the portfolio of government securities held by the central bank would be the object of partisan contention in this context. Purchases or sales in the open market are relatively clear signals of central bank intentions in money and credit markets. A sale of FNMA issues, bankers' acceptances, or Treasury notes could be interpreted as an endorsement or repudiation of the economic goals of a party or a president.

Harry S Truman knew that open market purchases of bonds were imperative for bond prices to remain stable. Dwight Eisenhower knew that open market purchases of bonds were imperative for simultaneous refunding of national debt and economic expansion. Lyndon Johnson knew that purchases of FNMA issues could save a faltering mortgage market. The FOMC rejected each of these appeals—transactions in the particular security was identified as inconsistent with the overall approach of the Fed to management of credit and capital markets. The intransigence of the FOMC during the Bills Only period foreclosed long-term debt financing absent congressional action to raise long-term rate ceilings. Changes in transactions rules affected the policy choices (and policy alternatives) of elected officials.

If the argument outlined for Arthur Burns in 1970 was correct, then open market operations in long-term securities, bankers acceptances, and agency issues mobilize particular interests (municipal governments, exporters, home builders) to directly pressure the Fed to buy particular types of securities. The broadening of Fed open market purchases seems to undercut Fed objectives related to autonomy. Under the broad rules adopted in 1966, transactions in particular types of securities have been directed at specific types of monetary and financial problems.

The broad rules that now govern transactions in the open market permit, but do not compel, the central bank to direct credit to particular segments of money and capital markets. The experimentation with broad purchases of agency issues in the early 1970s was conducted during a period when congressional initiatives threatened to explicitly assign the Fed the task of allocation of credit using the reserve requirement.[35] If economic interests representing agriculture, housing, or small business received permanent preferential treatment in the conduct of monetary policy by the central bank, the central bank loses both the discretion to distribute the burdens of monetary restraint and the formal ability to pursue the goal of price stability. Goodman (1992) describes a similar dilemma faced by decision makers in the German central bank in the 1970s. The *Bundesbank* tolerated high budget deficits rather than directly conflict with a coalition of business, labor and political leaders (the *Konzertierte Aktion*). Temporary accommodation was a price of long run autonomy. Prospectively, the decision by Arthur Burns to support the market for home mortgages with aggressive purchases of agency issues appears to commit the central bank to the type of credit allocation that invites political influence and control. Retrospectively, the influx of capital to the mortgage market in the early 1970s both broadened the secondary market for home mortgages (providing some protection against monetary restraint in the future) and weakened proposals for more direct and permanent allocation of credit by the central bank. The broadening of securities purchases is inconsistent with efforts to minimize the role of the Fed in credit allocation, but wholly consistent with the efforts of Arthur Burns and his contemporaries to avoid the politically impossible task of allocating credit across economic functions (home-building, business, government, agriculture).

Rules that affect the distribution of open market transactions across Treasury securities and agency issues are important variables that determine how the costs and benefits of monetary policy are distributed across money and capital markets. Restrictive rules like Bills Only and its derivatives are probably the best example of the trade-offs facing Fed decision makers confronted with distributive choices. Restrictive rules reduce precision of monetary control (and control over interest rates). But the restrictive rules also discourage active monitoring by legislators and the White House. Consider the case of the Bank of Canada. At the same time that the Fed experimented with Bills Only practices, the Bank of Canada adopted a completely different set of operating practices and rules (Chant and Acheson 1986). Bank of Canada operating procedures lowered Treasury financing costs by encouraging commercial banks to purchase government securities. This created a narrow securities market under fairly direct central bank control. The direct control strategy of the Bank of Canada highlighted the benefits of oversight and supervision to interested legislators. In contrast, the Fed created a broad market for government securities that extended the scope of the monetary policy conducted through the purchase and sale of public debt. The Fed created an indirect mechanism to transmit monetary policy to nonbank financial intermediaries. The indirect control strategy of the U.S. central bank creates obstacles for elected officials interested in using central bank instruments to affect the distribution of capital. Rules (and instrument choice) can increase control of central bankers over the allocation of credit only at the risk of attracting scrutiny from elected officials. In the case of the Fed, open market rules restricted the use of monetary policy instruments to allocate credit, minimizing incentives for political supervision in the crucial formative period of the autonomous Fed.

NOTES

1. For a discussion of the postwar funds market, see "*The Federal Funds Market—A Study by a Federal Reserve System Committee.*" Board of Governors of the Federal Reserve System. May 1959.

2. *Treasury-Federal Reserve Study of the Government Securities Market. 1959.* Part I. Section 2. Appendix A. Selected Background Material. History of Trading in U.S. Government Securities.

3. Memo. Bartelt to John Snyder. 12 February 1947. Folder: *Fiscal—financing. 1946-52 (Folder 2).* Box #15. Papers of John W. Snyder. Secretary of the Treasury. 1946-1952. Harry S Truman Library.

4. During the pegging period, yields on short-term securities were maintained at 7/8 percent, yields on certificates at 1 1/8, and Treasury bond yields were pegged at 2 1/2 percent.

5. Memo. Leon Keyserling and John Clark to the President. 11 April 1951. Folder: *Quarterly Report to the President—Supplements to First Quarter, 1951.* Papers of Leon Keyserling. Box #2. Harry S Truman Library.

6. Outstanding public debt totaled to over 250 billion dollars at the time, with individual investors holding 64 billion dollars, commercial banks holding 74 billion dollars, and the Federal Reserve System holding nearly 23 billion dollars (*Economic Report of the President,* 1950).

7. Quarterly Report to the President. First Quarter, 1947; First Quarter, 1948; First Quarter, 1951. Folder: *CEA: Report File, 1946-1953.* Papers of Leon Keyserling. Box #2. Harry S Truman Library.

8. Letter. President Truman to Thomas McCabe. 25 August 1950. *Subject File, Agencies, Federal Reserve Board. President's Secretary's File.* Box # 144. Papers of Harry S Truman. Harry S Truman Library.

9. Letter. John D. Clark to President Truman. 1 January 1949. Folder *OF-230 (1945-1948) (Banking)* Official Files. Papers of Harry S Truman. Harry S Truman Library

10. *Treasury-Federal Reserve Study of the Government Securities Market. 1959.* Part I. Section 2. Appendix A. Selected Background Material. History of Trading in U.S. Government Securities.

11. Memo. Bartelt, Fiscal Assistant Secretary, to John Snyder. 19 September 1950. Folder: *Federal Reserve Bank—Interest. 1948-50 (folder 2).* Box #14. Papers of John W. Snyder. Secretary of the Treasury. 1946-1952. Harry S Truman Library.

12. Memo. Clark to Murphy. 4 April 1951. Folder. *CEA.* Files of Charles S. Murphy. Papers of Harry S Truman. Box #21. Harry S Truman Library.

13. Robert Roosa Interview. Oral History. Dwight D. Eisenhower Library.

14. The Transition to Free Markets. Address of William Martin before the Economic Club of Detroit. Reprinted in the *Federal Reserve Bulletin.* April 1953.

15. Letter. Arthur Burns to L.W. Douglas. 17 Sept 1956. Folder: *Fiscal and Monetary—Miscellaneous Correspondence re the Economy, 1956.* Box #107. Series VII. CEA. Papers of Arthur Burns. Dwight D. Eisenhower Library.

16. Memo. Paul McCracken to the CEA. 24 September 1956. Folder: *Fiscal and Monetary: Can Inflation Be Stopped?* Box #107. Papers of Arthur Burns. Dwight D. Eisenhower Library.

17. AFB Talk. 16 November 1956. Folder: *Talk on Credit Restraint, Given at Cabinet Mting.* Box #76. Papers of Arthur F. Burns. Dwight D. Eisenhower Library.

18. Letter. Sherman Adams to Governor Collins. 14 Jan 1957. Folder: *OF 115C. Credit.* White House Central Files. Official Files. Box #566. Dwight D. Eisenhower Library.

19. Memo. Marshall Kaplan to the Council. 11 October 1956. Comments for the Economic Report. Folder: *Fiscal and Monetary—Financial Reports, 1956 (1).* Series VII. CEA. Box #106. Papers of Arthur Burns. Dwight D. Eisenhower Library.

20. Memo. Raymond Saulnier to Sherman Adams. 20 Dec 1957. Folder: *CEA*. Confidential Files. Box #18. White House Central Files. Dwight D. Eisenhower Library.

21. Memo. Aubrey Langston to the FOMC. 10 Dec 1953. Folder: *Federal Reserve Board Correspondence, 1953*. Papers of Arthur Burns. Box #98. Dwight D. Eisenhower Library.

22. Memo. Winfield Riefler to Gabriel Hauge. 13 December 1954. Folder: *OF-14, Federal Reserve System (1).* White House Central Files. Official Files. Dwight D. Eisenhower Library.

23. Capital market segmentation and the real effects of intervention in capital markets are discussed briefly in Chapter 7.

24. Memo. Neil Jacoby to Gabriel Hauge. 9 August 1954. Folder: *Fiscal and Monetary- Stabilization Planning Committee.* Papers of Arthur Burns. Series VII. CEA. Box #108. Dwight D. Eisenhower Library.

25. Paper. Debt Management during Calendar Year 1954. By Neil Jacoby. 2 March 1954. Folder: *Debt Management 1954*. Files of the Office of the CEA, 1953-1961. Box #9. Dwight D. Eisenhower Library.

26. Memo. Raymond Saulnier to Sherman Adams. 20 December 1957. Folder: *CEA*. Confidential Files Box #18. White House Central Files. Dwight D. Eisenhower Library.

27. Paper. Data Analysis Staff. Department of the Treasury. 23 May 1958. Folder: *Anderson, Robert B. (2).* Ann Whitman File. Administration Series. Box #2. Dwight D. Eisenhower Library.

28. Bond Interest Rates. *1959 Congressional Quarterly Almanac.* Washington, D.C.: Congressional Quarterly News Features. (273)

29. Memo. Office of the Secretary to the Board of Governors. 3 November 1970. Folder: *Bankers' Acceptances. Federal Reserve Board Subject File.* Box # B7. Papers of Arthur Burns. Gerald R. Ford Library.

30. Memo. Raymond Saulnier to President Eisenhower. 1 Jan 1961. Folder: *Economic Policy, Memoranda on, 1952-1961 (4).* Papers of Raymond Saulnier. Box #7. Dwight D. Eisenhower Library.

31. Memo. Ackley to President Johnson. 1 Jan 1967. Folder: *FG 233 EX.* FG SERIES. Box #282. White House Central Files. Lyndon Baines Johnson Library.

32. Memo. Axilrod to Arthur Burns. 5 Feb 1970. Folder: *Purchase of Agency Issues.* Box #B91. Arthur Burns Papers. Gerald R. Ford Library.

33. The Economic Reports of the President (Various Years) describe the distribution of outstanding government debt across commercial banks, miscellaneous investors, and the Federal Reserve System. Fed holdings of FNMA debt increased dramatically in the 1970s, indicating active open market purchase of FNMA issues.

34. Annual open market activity is summarized in each *Annual Report of the Board of Governors of the Federal Reserve System.* Data from the annual reports are used in Figure 4 and other descriptions of annual open market transactions. Quarterly open market activity is reported in financial market flow of funds data distributed by the Federal Reserve System. Data from the flow of funds are used in Figure 7. The organization and contents of the flow of funds data are reported in the *Flow of Funds Coded Tables, Z.1 and C.9 releases, Monthly domestic nonfinancial debt.* Board of Governors of the Federal Reserve System: Washington D.C. (September 1993). The data used for the figures are from the *Flow of Funds diskettes* produced by the Board of Governors in 1993. The Flow of Funds diskettes contain quarterly data from the Federal Reserve Board's *Z.1 (Flows and Outstandings) release.* The structure and concepts used to aggregate and report the flow of funds are described in the *Introduction to the Flow of Funds.* Board of Governors of the Federal Reserve System: Washington D.C. (June 1980).

35. See Chapter 3 for details on reserve requirements on assets and the testimony of Andrew Brimmer on central bank allocation of capital.

CHAPTER 5

Selective Credit Controls and Credit Allocation

In addition to open market transactions and reserve requirements, the Fed has directly controlled terms of the end use of credit to implement monetary policy. Direct allocation of capital was perceived as essential for the conduct of macroeconomic stabilization policy following World War II. Postwar demand for consumer durable goods, constrained by rationing and diversion of critical materials to war production, was expected to lead to large increases in production, consumer lending, and, ultimately, price levels. To reduce demand and stabilize production activity, decision makers at the Board of Governors implemented a regime of direct selective controls that limited credit and capital for consumers. Later, during mobilization for the Korean War, the Fed administered no less than four sets of direct selective controls on credit and capital. Regulation W specified the terms of consumer installment credit (at the major appliance level). Regulation X specified the terms of real estate mortgages. Regulation T governed the terms of bank credit for transactions in securities and common stock. Regulation Q specified the maximum amount of interest payable by commercial banks on demand and time deposits. The terms of credit extension for stock market transactions remain in force today; the other regulations have been rescinded. The abrupt termination of selective controls in the 1950s is consistent with other procedural choices made at the Fed after World War II. Direct selective controls invited organized opposition to monetary policy choices of the Board of Governors. Direct controls were a direct threat to Fed autonomy.

The repudiation of direct selective controls is somewhat puzzling given the enthusiastic administration and endorsement of direct controls before 1950. The termination of selective controls on consumer credit after the Korean mobilization was an unanticipated outcome of the political conflicts between lenders and the monetary authority during the mobilization period. Contemporary observers concluded that the demise of these visible selective controls was a consequence of vocal opposition by the affected interests, rather than widespread popular opposition, insurmountable enforcement problems, or economic evidence of the failure of the controls (Shay 1953, Ahearn 1963). The economic and credit market problems that led many economists and central bankers to endorse selective controls were not contained before the direct selective controls were terminated. The rapid growth of consumer installment credit and expansion of bank credit remained problematic for members of the Board of Governors well after 1950.

The termination of direct and selective controls narrowed the scope of alternatives for elected officials interested in preserving credit for some economic functions and limiting credit for others. The original Federal Reserve Act anticipated allocation of credit according to social needs and efficiency criteria, but the decision makers in the postwar Fed embraced only very indirect mechanisms to allocate credit. As a substitute for Fed action, elected officials have proposed a variety of statutory rules to manage the distribution of monetary restraint in the absence of direct selective controls. Policy makers in the Fed have revealed an unambiguous preference for rules that only indirectly influence financial market outcomes and rules that minimize political conflict over credit market outcomes. Since direct selective controls produce vocal opposition, they are undesirable. The economic merits or drawbacks of direct controls do not explain either the persistence or termination of particular controls.

ADMINISTRATION OF DIRECT SELECTIVE CONTROLS

Direct Credit Regulation and Credit Allocation

The original charter of the Fed specifically directed the monetary authority to regulate the end use of credit in order to direct capital toward productive enterprise and discourage the use of credit for speculation. The theoretical basis for central bank activity before 1920 (commercial loan theory) assumed that the "quality of credit" and not the simply the "quantity of money" should guide central bank provision of reserves and rediscounting facilities (Chandler 1970). It was assumed that if speculative and non-productive uses of credit were eliminated, then the remaining volume of credit would naturally reflect the actual needs of the economy. The regulation of credit end use to achieve these ends was undertaken by the regional Reserve Banks in the Federal Reserve System. The Reserve Banks established discount window borrowing standards that induced banks to restrict particular types of lending in exchange for borrowing (rediscounting) privileges. This qualitative allocation of credit was intended to be a substitute for quantitative rules that would link the volume of credit to economic indicators such as the level of prices (Annual Report of the Board of Governors 1923, 31-33).

The ability of the regional Reserve Banks to control the end use of credit was undone by a dramatic drop in Reserve Bank lending after 1934. Alternative inexpensive sources of funds made discounting unattractive for commercial banks, so commercial banks could acquire unrestricted capital from other sources and ignore the borrowing standards imposed by the Reserve Banks. Direct regulation of credit for the purchase of common stock (1934) and the regulation of consumer credit (1941) were originally intended to satisfy the credit quality objectives that the discount lending function could no longer meet. Direct controls on the extension of credit have historically been used by central banks to both regulate the demand for credit over the business cycle and direct the end use of credit toward productive enterprise. Adoption of direct controls on consumer credit in particular was consistent with broader attitudes about profligate consumer expenditures and the moral imperative of thrift in the 1920s and 1930s (Kubik, 1996). Consumer instalment financing plans were believed to be destructive of both personal moral welfare and aggregate savings.

After World War II, the Fed continued to intervene in money and financial markets by regulating the terms and maturity of obligations incurred by debtors to make purchases in various markets. These regulations influenced the demand for credit among prospective buyers by making terms of credit most attractive when markets were poor (during recessions, for example) and making terms of credit less attractive when markets were robust. The regulation of particular sectors of the credit market was not an unusual extension of the authority of the Board of Governors or an anomaly of wartime mobilization, but instead part of an ongoing strategy to adopt particular and selective instruments that could substitute for the discount mechanism and prevent use of credit for speculative and non-productive needs. It is in this context—the active experimentation with substitutes for rediscounting—that the Fed adopted a variety of selective controls that produced vocal opposition from affected nonbank lenders. The policy failures of the Great Depression motivated Congress to formally restructure the Federal Reserve System and substantially amend the Federal Reserve Act. Innovations in economic theories of both consumer behavior and money and banking also contributed to experimentation with new rules and instruments. The political implications of the new approaches, especially after the urgency of wartime mobilization and production subsided, were apparently not well understood at the time. The qualitative allocation of credit through rediscounting (the prewar convention) confined the effects of monetary policy choices to the voluntary members of the Fed. Wartime direct selective controls extended regulation and credit allocation to all lenders. Experience across a number of selective instruments revealed a host of political problems with direct selective controls.

Regulation W: Regulation of Consumer Installment Credit after World War II

The Annual Reports of the Board of Governors of the Federal Reserve System for 1945 and 1946 requested permanent statutory authority for the Fed to regulate consumer installment credit:

> Over past 30 years, consumer installment financing has come to occupy an important and strategic place in the national economy. Such financing is essential to the mass distribution and consequently the mass production of consumers' durable goods. From time to time however, the expansion and subsequent expansion of consumer credit have gone so far as to accentuate the upswings and downswings of the business cycle. *There is no way of preventing such excessive expansion and contraction except governmental regulation* of the terms on which consumer credit shall be made available, . . . [1]

In the first quarterly report of the CEA to the president, the Council also advocated permanent statutory authority for the Board of Governors of the Federal Reserve System to regulate the terms of consumer installment credit.[2] The recommendation was included in the Economic Report of the President again in 1948.

Truman and his CEA envisioned selective credit controls as the keystone of Fed monetary restraint.[3] Consumer installment credit was the fastest growing segment of the money and capital markets immediately after World War II. Regulation of the terms of installment credit had two objectives. The primary objective of the regulation was to restrain growing demands for consumer durables and automobiles to conserve critical materials needed for defense production. The second objective was to smooth fluctuations in consumer installment credit outlays in order to stabilize the economy over the business cycle (Shay 1953).

Opposition from outside of the central bank to the continuing regulation of consumer installment credit began soon after the end of World War II. The Retail Credit Institute, as well other trade associations representing lenders, demanded that the White House terminate direct controls. Shay (1953) identifies a variety of opponents including the ABA, American Finance Congress, Consumer Bankers Association, National Automobile Dealers Association, and the National Consumer Finance Association. Despite this vocal opposition, Chairman Marriner Eccles chose to advocate selective controls on consumer credit as a permanent instrument. He explained the System position for a Massachusetts official in 1947:

> On the other hand, we have not had any protests against the regulation from consumer groups and an impressive array of informed, impartial economic opinion agrees with the view that restraints upon the expansion of consumer credit would be in the interests of the country from the long-range standpoint.[4]

Jake Vardeman, a Truman appointee to the Board of Governors of the Federal Reserve System, was the only opponent of selective credit controls on the FOMC in late 1940s. In correspondence with Truman, Vardeman argued that the president should terminate consumer credit controls implemented under Executive Order. He suggested that Truman should force Congress to address the need for selective controls and force Congress to face rising political opposition.[5] The remaining members of the Board of Governors supported the extension of Regulation W under Executive Order (and even permanent statutory authority for Board regulation). It was made clear to Truman that the Board of Governors would accept the White House position in any case. Specifically, Truman was informed that "the Board would like an opportunity to recommend the action the President desires."[6]

The Truman White House at first elected to allow consumer credit regulation to expire in 1947. The White House strategy was to compel Congress to enact permanent statutory authority for the Fed to regulate credit demand.[7] Although Congress failed to pass legislation explicitly authorizing the regulation of consumer credit, Regulation W remained in force while Congress considered other anti-inflation measures. The controls were allowed to formally expire in 1949, despite evidence of effective restraint of the growth of consumer installment credit (Ahearn 1963). One contemporary observer concluded:

> The Federal Reserve authorities, on the basis of their experience with the regulation during these years, felt there was a need for what was termed a reasonable regulation of consumer installment credit on a continuing basis. However, the opposition to the continuation of the regulation was too well organized, and with the lapse of inflationary pressures Regulation W was allowed to expire once again on June 30, 1949 (Shay 1953, 87).

In a fairly brief period of experience, less than six years after World War II, the political consequences of selective credit controls began to undermine support for direct selective intervention within the Board of Governors of the Federal Reserve System. Direct selective controls mobilize political opposition from a variety of economic sectors, inviting congressional specification of the timing, scope, and exceptions that are included in the regulations.

Direct Controls and the Mortgage Market

Members of the Board of Governors and the FOMC struggled with the theoretical utility and practical limitations of direct controls throughout the Truman Administration. The Board of Governors administered two distinct sets of direct controls under the Defense Production Act of 1950: controls on credit for real estate transactions and controls on consumer installment credit. Experience with Regulation X, controls on credit for real estate transactions, was disappointing. The postwar mortgage market was by far the largest sector of the money and capital markets. Over $80 billion in home mortgages were financed in the decade after World War II, accounting for nearly 50% of the total capital market flow of funds (Klaman 1961). Despite the large size of the market, or perhaps because of the large size, the Board of Governors of the Federal Reserve System opposed legislation that would compel the Federal Reserve Banks to regulate the terms of mortgage credit. Even while the Board of Governors was requesting permanent authority to regulate the terms of consumer installment credit, the Board consistently opposed real estate credit controls as an administrative nightmare. Chairman Marriner Eccles specifically objected to real estate credit regulation in testimony to Congress in 1947.[8] At the time that real estate selective controls were considered for the central bank, other federal agencies were engaged in a massive campaign to provide low cost credit to home buyers. There was little urgency to make selective regulation of mortgage terms a permanent instrument of the monetary authority. Public and congressional preferences for easy credit for veterans coupled with extraordinary demand for new housing made it unlikely that direct regulation would be popular.

During the Korean mobilization, the Fed did choose to intervene and apply restraint to mortgage markets. The restraint was part of a coordinated campaign across a number of federal regulators. The Board of Governors adopted Regulation X as a complement to general monetary restraint implemented by the FOMC and administrative restraint of mortgage guarantees by the Federal National Mortgage Association and the Federal Housing Administration. Regulation X stipulated the minimum down payment and loan-to-value amounts for residential home mortgages. The specific objective of the regulation was to reduce the demand for mortgage credit and free building materials and labor for the Korean war effort. Regulation X was initiated in October 1950 and rescinded entirely in September 1953. The real effects of the selective restraint on mortgage lending activity were, according to most published accounts, ambiguous (Ahearn 1963).

Despite the volatility and size of the residential mortgage markets, there have been no attempts to introduce direct selective controls on the terms of mortgage credit since the Korean War. The Federal Housing Administration and Veterans Administration continue to provide direct support for mortgage lending and support the secondary market for home mortgages on a counter-cyclical basis. The use of selective controls to restrain mortgage markets, after a period of stimulus initiated by government action, would place the Fed in direct conflict with the interests of home buyers, home builders, and bank financial institutions prepared to make mortgage loans. These are precisely the types of political conflicts that decision makers in the Fed seek to avoid. Consistent with the strategy of increasing autonomy from political actors and groups, decision makers in the Fed do not endorse reliance on direct controls as instruments of monetary policy. Members of Congress, typically responsive to these same groups and actors, do not compel the Fed to undertake the direct allocation or regulation of credit for purposes of implementing monetary restraint.

Credit Controls After Regulation W

The CEA under Truman remained an advocate of selective controls even after the Accord with the Treasury made clear the preferences of the Fed for primary reliance on open market operations rather than selective controls.[9] For some time, the Board of Governors of the Federal Reserve System remained divided over the utility of selective controls. Jake Vardeman continued to campaign against selective controls throughout his tenure on the Board of Governors. In 1951, he specified his objections for Treasury Secretary John Snyder:

> In other words, distrust and loss of confidence in the Board's objectivity brought about by these pinpoint, annoying, and ineffective selective controls potentially weaken the entire structure of Board authority. I have always thought that the Board's contribution would be more effective if the Board were more exclusively in the position of a High Court and less in the position of a police judge and policeman.[10]

Vardeman also documented his reservations for the financial press:

> Factional opposition to these controls, some sound and some selfish, handicaps the overall monetary and credit control functions of the Federal Reserve System because when the Board acts in these

> limited areas the populace and the congressional opposition become vocal and strong enough to prevent the Board being granted necessary additional selective and general credit control authority to meet its contemplated statutory responsibility in the money and credit field.[11]

There were a number of decision makers in the Fed that did not share Vardeman's position. After the Treasury Accord in 1951, selective controls were defended as a vital component of a flexible monetary policy by a number of powerful actors in the Fed—including the Chairman of the Board of Governors, William Martin, and New York Reserve Bank President Allan Sproul. Martin advocated selective controls on consumer installment credit in a widely publicized speech before a Conference of Leading Automobile Finance Companies in 1953.[12] As late as 1955 Sproul concluded that direct selective controls on consumer credit were necessary to avoid destabilizing spending patterns during the turns of the business cycle (Ritter 1980). Testifying before a Senate Committee in 1957, Chairman William Martin suggested that premature termination of Regulation W in 1952 contributed to problems with inflation in succeeding quarters—confirming the suspicion among members of Congress that the Fed could effectively use selective controls to manage inflation.[13]

Reserve Bank President Allan Sproul later described the Board position on consumer credit controls in 1953 as "irresolution bordering on timidity" (Ritter 1980). In early 1956 the Chairman of the CEA, Arthur Burns, again advocated permanent statutory authority for the regulation of consumer installment credit.[14] The Eisenhower White House staff chose to await the publication of an Fed exhaustive study on the control of consumer installment credit before acting on the CEA recommendation. The 1957 study dismissed consumer credit controls as an unnecessary supplement to general monetary restraint. The report identified consumer credit fluctuations as an important component of stabilization problems in the mid-1950s, but rejected selective controls as the solution.[15] After cabinet-level deliberations the Eisenhower Administration endorsed the conclusions of the study and abandoned proposed regulations of consumer credit. The Board never implemented controls on consumer installment credit after 1952, despite considerable study of the prospective effects of proposed controls. The failure to resume controls on consumer installment credit is particularly puzzling, given the recent apparent success of selective controls during the war (Ahearn 1963).

The Eisenhower recommendations did not end White House infatuation with selective regulation of consumer credit as an instrument of inflation control. Advisors to Lyndon Johnson, Richard Nixon, and Gerald Ford each studied the administrative and legal feasibility of direct controls on consumer credit. Assistant Attorney General William Rehnquist concluded that President Nixon retained the implicit authority to initiate direct controls (specifically, Regulation W) under the national state of emergency declared by Harry Truman in 1950.[16] The ambiguous language used by Congress after World War II to rescind, yet not permanently foreclose, regulation of consumer credit (a 1947 Joint Resolution) provided the authority for executive action. Nixon also received explicit legislative authority for direct presidential allocation of credit (to be administered by the Fed) under the Credit Control Act of 1969. The Fed was never compelled to implement selective regulations of consumer installment credit under the 1969 Act. Instead, the Fed positively responded to White House and congressional demands for selective application of monetary restraint by implementing less direct methods of selective restraint: voluntary restraint programs and supervisory suasion.

EXPERIMENTATION WITH INDIRECT CREDIT CONTROLS

The rejection of selective controls by the central bank after 1952 cannot be interpreted as evidence of central bank complacency about the growth of installment credit or the overall distribution of capital and credit. The Board of Governors simply chose to use different instruments to allocate credit across economic sectors. The alternative instruments, typically designated as "covert controls," included supervisory suasion, manipulation of discount window lending practices, and (less covertly) the administration of voluntary restraint programs. These covert controls preserve discretion for the central bank to distribute the burdens of monetary restraint to various economic sectors without creating specific incentives for elected officials to use legislation to influence that distribution.

Each of the covert controls adopted by the central bank affected the distribution of credit through bank financial institutions, but did not extend regulation to nonbank financial institutions. Commercial bank compliance with central bank goals is contingent upon either membership in the Federal Reserve System or participation in a voluntary program. Thus commercial banks always have an inexpensive noncompliance option. Withdrawal from the Fed can substitute for political opposition to the redistributive goals of the central bank. Covert controls that target System members or are strictly voluntary reduce the probability of conflict between affected economic interests and the central bank. Each of three types of "covert" or indirect controls were used to pursue distributive objectives with a minimum of scrutiny from Congress. After World War II, the Board of Governors of the Federal Reserve System alternately relied on voluntary restraint programs, discount window non-price rationing, and supervisory suasion.

Supervisory Suasion

Bank examination and supervisory responsibilities give the monetary authority (and other financial regulatory agencies) considerable discretion in the evaluation of lending practices of banks. The practice of warning lenders to avoid specific lending practices—generous consumer credit installment plans, lending to foreign clients, forward commitments to business—allows bank regulatory authorities to influence bank lending decisions without resorting to direct controls. Described as "moral suasion" or "supervisory suasion," these indirect mechanisms are used by central banks in most countries. Chant and Acheson (1972) argue that central bankers strictly prefer these mechanisms to direct controls for a number of reasons. First, supervisory suasion can be undertaken without specific statutory approval. Commercial bank lending guidelines are routinely updated to reflect changes in technology and commercial bank practices, so administrative discretion over lending guidelines is quite broad. Second, the results of changes in lending guidelines are easily reversible. If the regulations do not have the desired effect or the policy objectives of the regulation are quickly accomplished, the lending guidelines can be quickly updated. Finally, the public rarely pays close attention to the standards used by bank supervisors to evaluate the financial positions of banks. Indirect mechanisms give central bankers substantial discretion over the distribution of monetary restraint across specific segments of money and capital markets.

Experience with supervisory suasion has been fairly extensive. Supervisory suasion was used early in the Eisenhower administration in a coordinated campaign to slow the growth of particular forms of consumer installment credit and later under the Johnson administration to discourage forward commitments from banks to prime business customers. Subsequent administrations have also turned to supervisory suasion in an effort to shift the burden of monetary restraint from one sector of the economy to another. In a notable display of supervisory scrutiny, the Board of Governors of the Federal Reserve System and the Federal Advisory Council published general guidelines directing banks to engage in "appropriate" lending practices during the period of high credit demand in 1974.[17]

Early efforts to slow the growth of installment credit highlight the utility of the indirect approach to credit allocation. The Council of Economic Advisors and the Advisory Board on Economic Growth and Stability (ABEGS) concluded in early 1956 that the terms of credit for installment financing were becoming generous to the point of endangering economic and price stability. The solution—to be jointly implemented by the Federal Deposit Insurance Corporation, the Comptroller of the Currency, and the Board of Governors of the Federal Reserve System—was to inform banks that supervisory agencies would consider installment credit lending practices when evaluating bank performance and determining eligibility for discount facilities.[18] The Comptroller of the Currency and the Board of Governors prepared and delivered letters to the banks under their jurisdiction, although the Comptroller in particular had reservations about the practice of setting explicit lending standards.[19] The FDIC chose not to issue a similar letter to banks participating in the federal deposit insurance program and the White House admonished the agency:

> We have felt that some action was called for in the field of consumer installment credit, though this is an area in which the Federal Government under existing law can do little more than to exercise moral suasion over lenders.
>
> It is regrettable that your letter [to field examiners] not only fails to express any concern over automobile credit developments, but explicitly states that the Corporation feels no serious concern over the trend of installment credit terms.[20]

Supervisory suasion, implemented effectively, can have the same economic effects as direct regulation. But the political consequences of supervisory suasion are quite different from the consequences of direct regulation. Political opposition to selective restraint is diffused across the various bank regulators rather than concentrated upon the Board of Governors of the Federal Reserve System. If a number of federal agencies are enlisted to restrain the flow of credit to a particular sector of the economy, the chance that the Fed will come under direct congressional scrutiny or control is quite rare. Using supervisory suasion in concert with other regulators, the central bank can apply monetary restraint to consumer installment lending, but at the same time avoid the kinds of specific and controversial choices that accompany direct regulation of the terms of credit. As the exclusive arbiter of direct controls, congressional action to affect Fed decisions is highly likely. If Fed decision makers seek to actively avoid scrutiny from Congress and value central bank autonomy, then reliance on supervisory suasion or moral suasion is not surprising.

Discount Window Non-Price Rationing

Discount window loans are typically a last resort for commercial banks seeking funds to meet reserve deficiencies. The regional reserve banks of the Fed grant discount window loans to banks unable to meet reserve requirements with conventional sources of funds. Changes in the interest rate charged for window lending (the discount rate) are among the most controversial actions taken by the Board of Governors of the Federal Reserve System. Discount rate ceilings were an explicit provision of the 1951 Treasury Accord. Unexpected changes in the discount rate at critical moments infuriated Dwight Eisenhower (April 1956) and Lyndon Johnson (December 1965). Unanticipated upward adjustments in the discount rate have been the catalyst for reform proposals from the White House to compel Fed responsiveness to executive demands.

Simple administrative restrictions on access to discount window funds, although common, have not attracted the same types of public scrutiny or controversy as changes in the price of discount window funds. Individual Reserve Banks have the discretion to selectively suspend discount window borrowing privileges of member banks that either abuse the lending privilege or appear to deviate from acceptable commercial lending practices. If a Reserve Bank announces that a particular lending practice has become unacceptable, then commercial banks could jeopardize borrowing privileges by refusing to amend lending practices. If a commercial bank requires frequent and substantial access to discount funds in order to meet unexpected changes in reserve needs, then the bank must conform to the lending practices prescribed by the Fed. These lending criteria receive little scrutiny from members of Congress or the financial press. Policy makers in the Fed use the lending criteria to target particular borrowers for application of monetary restraint.

The Board of Governors of the Federal Reserve System announced important changes in rules governing discount window lending during the Eisenhower Administration. The amended rules were intended to reflect the subordination of discount window borrowing to open market operations for the purpose of implementing domestic monetary policy. In early 1965 the Fed began a study of discount window lending administration designed to address decreases in borrowing from the reserve banks under the new rules. Discount window borrowing reached unparalleled lows during the early 1960s, limiting the extent to which the Fed could influence bank lending practices through the non-price rationing of discount window funds. Figure 8 displays the proportion of reserves borrowed through the discount window between 1945 and 1990.

After discount window borrowing exceed three percent of total reserves in 1966, the White House encouraged the Fed to use discount window privileges to induce commercial banks to restrict business loans. The Chairman of the CEA described the practice of discount window rationing at the Fed:

> The Fed today raised the reserves that it requires banks to hold against time deposits. But it did so in such a way that mainly hits the big banks that issue most of the CDs.
>
> They may dump some municipals. But many of them will be forced into the Fed's discount window. This is what the Fed wants.
>
> When they do come in, the Fed will force them to ration their loans to their big customers at the price of getting accommodation. This is the strategy we have been urging on the Fed for months.[21]

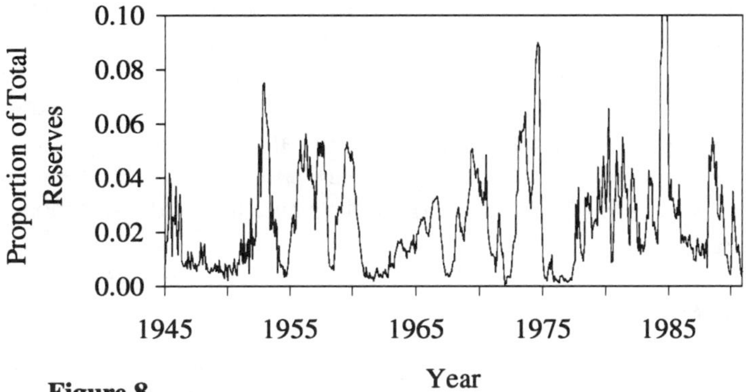

Figure 8
Discount window borrowing as a proportion of total reserves (1945-1990).

Source: Federal Reserve Economic Data, Federal Reserve Bank of St. Louis

The rationing measures were not very effective. Higher reserve requirements encouraged banks to seek alternative sources of funds rather than borrow from the Reserve Banks. This unanticipated failure led to a rehabilitation of discount window lending procedures in the late 1960s.[22] Uniform discount window lending procedures were initiated at the Reserve Banks with the explicit goal of developing commercial bank ties to Reserve Banks by increasing discount window borrowing.[23] These narrow changes in the administration of discount window borrowing practices in July 1968 signaled a broader role for discount window borrowing in the Fed. Over time, the level of borrowing has increased.

If bank borrowing from the discount window could be encouraged, then the Reserve Banks could exert greater control over bank lending practices of discount window borrowers. The rehabilitation of the discount mechanism was intended to facilitate the types of distributive actions that require commercial banks to expand or contract lending to particular economic sectors. A 1971 System study suggested that consideration be given to the use of the discount mechanism to provide "long-term credit to meet the needs of banks servicing perennial credit-deficit areas or sectors."[24] From the perspective of central bankers, discount window rationing appears to have the same political benefits of supervisory suasion. Opposition to central bank policies are confined to voluntary member banks. Specific congressional instructions regarding discounting or permanent institutional protection for particular economic sectors at the discount window have never been observed. Greater reliance upon the discount mechanism increases central bank discretion to distribute the burdens of monetary restraint.

Voluntary Restraint Programs

As a substitute for formal direct control programs, voluntary credit restraint programs have targeted specific categories of lending as undesirable: loans to support municipal expenditures and credit to business during the Truman administration, mortgage lending during the Eisenhower Administration, and the extension of credit to foreign borrowers during the Johnson Administration. In each case, members of the Board of Governors were attempting to affect the flow of capital across borrowers. Instead of rationing credit through increasing interest rates or directly regulating the terms for borrowers, banks were asked to voluntarily reduce loans to particular types of borrowers. The real effects of the programs were mixed.

In 1951 the Board of Governors of the Federal Reserve System implemented a voluntary restraint program directed at financial institutions to encourage lending to meet the "essential needs of agriculture, industry, and commerce" while at the same time restraining inflation and restricting the expansion of bank credit.[25] The main objective of the program was to slow the expansion of bank credit loaned to business.[26] Regional committees reviewed specific proposed commercial bank loans to determine if the end use of credit did in fact meet essential needs. The regional committees also had the authority to instruct commercial banks to refuse to bid on securities issued by state and local governments. Particularly controversial were decisions by a West Virginia regional committee to withdraw support for bonds used to finance support payments to veterans—a program mandated in an amendment to the State constitution.[27] Although compliance with the decisions of the committees were voluntary and the involvement of the Board of Governors in the regional committees was minimal, the administration of the program by the Fed attracted considerable attention from organized interests and the White House. After a regional committee blocked bank support for municipal works projects in the State of Washington, the White House directed that the voluntary restraint program exempt loans to municipal and state governments from the screening process.[28] The program was terminated by the Board of Governors in May 1952, one month after the White House intervention. Although there was no formal (public) link between the two actions, the creation of political exemptions for certain classes of credit clearly undermined the restraint effort. The direct control program, although strictly voluntary, eventually triggered intervention by Congress and the White House. As soon as the Fed discretion was challenged, the program was terminated.

The Johnson White House initiated a voluntary program (VFCR) to restrain bank lending from large banks to foreign borrowers. The Chairman of the CEA, Gardner Ackley, explained to Johnson that a voluntary program could prevent the need for tight money in the domestic economy by shifting the burden of restraint to foreign borrowers. Ackley explained the details for Johnson:

> The Fed can set up a quantitative guideline for each bank, backed up by various controls (including especially the discount privilege) and by its detailed and frequent report of foreign loans.
>
> Confidential conversations with the New York Federal Reserve convince us that they know how to run a "moral suasion" policy. But Bill Martin must take the lead. *I think it is important that you talk to him about his role in making moral suasion on the banks really effective.*[29]

The voluntary program was administered by the Fed through the end of 1973. A Johnson appointee to the Board of Governors of the Federal Reserve System, Andrew Brimmer, suggested that the VFCR should serve as a model for later legislative proposals to allocate credit across money and capital markets. The program demonstrated how central bank suasion and guidelines could reduce the growth of credit in particular economic sectors. Arthur Burns, responding to the Brimmer testimony, explained why the VFCR program should be considered unique:

> It applied only to lending and investment by U.S. banks' domestic offices and exempted their foreign branches. Also, the program involved only bank credit extended to foreigners. Moreover, it involved very little differentiation among social goals or among corresponding categories of credit use.[30]

The burdens of restraint associated with the VFCR program were directed at foreign clients of U.S. banks, rather than domestic borrowers that could complain to members of Congress about the hardships of monetary restraint. Burns is correct that the program did not explicitly discriminate among domestic credit end uses. The effects of restraint were simply transferred to foreign economic sectors that cannot mobilize political support for exemption from monetary restraint. Application of monetary restraint with a selective instrument invites political opposition. The use of selective controls that do not punish domestic economic sectors is consistent with a strategy of instrument selection that minimizes political conflict over the distributive effects of monetary policy choices.

PERSISTENT SELECTIVE CONTROLS

After the economic crises of the 1930s, two sets of selective regulations were delegated (in part) to the Fed: selective controls designed to limit speculation in the stock market and selective controls designed to prevent destructive competition between financial institutions. These selective controls are extremely persistent and have typically been exempted from the arguments used by members of the Board of Governors to oppose selective controls on other market transactions.

Margin Requirements (Regulations T, G and U)

Margin requirements, selective credit controls on the extension of credit for the purchase of stocks and securities, have persisted since the 1930s with little resistance from the Fed or the industries affected by the regulations. Margin requirements are an idiosyncratic footnote to the canonical Fed position on markets and market mechanisms. For no other set of market transactions must an external authority specify the type (cash) or amount (varying percentage) of collateral necessary for a lender to advance money to a borrower. In the early 1950s, incoming Chairman William Martin described for various audiences the virtues of free market mechanisms and lamented prospective intervention of the government in transactions between buyers and sellers of automobiles, government securities, and commodities. Margin requirements were treated as an exception; these requirements, it was argued, performed a valuable and essential "social" function—dampening stock market fluctuations by discouraging (at appropriate times) excessive speculation in stocks and securities.

Rarely subjected to rigorous scrutiny by economists, the real effects of margin regulations are not entirely clear. Goldberg (1985) argues that firms offset the effects of margin regulations, sometimes resulting in market outcomes inconsistent with the objectives of the regulation. Despite these ambiguities, elected officials have historically demanded increases in the margin requirements when stock market prices appear to be rising at a rapid rate. Bibby and Davidson (1967) concluded that margin requirements were adjusted upwards (to a historic high of ninety percent) to satisfy congressional demands for stock market stability in the late 1950s. The CEA has also advocated increases in margin requirements as an early measure to control inflation under both Republican and Democratic presidents. Political controversy over margin requirements has been unremarkable, although the Fed has at times been criticized for not acting rapidly enough to prevent upward swings in stock prices. Margin requirements have remained fairly steady (at fifty percent) since 1974.

Interest Rate Ceilings (Regulation Q)

Regulation Q specified ceilings for the amount of interest payable on demand and time deposits at commercial banks. The regulation, authorized in the Banking Act of 1935, was intended to reduce price competition among commercial banks for customer deposits. The ceilings were not important competitive restraints before the mid-1950s. Interest rates offered by financial institutions such as mutual savings banks and thrift institutions remained well below the ceilings imposed on commercial banks. As interest rates on short-term money market instruments rose sharply in the early 1960s, the regulations became more controversial. During the Johnson Administration, Chairman William Martin argued that the regulatory ceilings were interfering with the flow of funds into savings. The solution proposed by the Board of Governors was higher ceilings coupled with a higher discount rate for borrowing from the Fed.[31]

Instead of removing the ceilings, the scope of interest rate ceilings was extended considerably in 1966 under the Interest Rate Adjustment Act. The regulations were applied to a wide variety of money market instruments and financial institutions. The extension was justified as a way to prevent interest rate competition for savings in forms other than demand and time deposits (mainly, Certificates of Deposit). Discretionary action taken by the Board of Governors and the Federal Home Loan Bank Board under the new act was considered a turning point in the administration of Regulation Q. First, the ceilings were administered in way that directed credit to thrift institutions (and the mortgage market). Second, ceilings were treated as a monetary policy instrument. The ceilings were intended to slow the rate of growth in bank credit.[32] Major proponents of the new authority (and the hidden hand behind the legislative initiative) was the National Association of Home Builders.[33] The results of the new Regulation Q ceilings were very disappointing. It was immediately recognized that the ceilings simply induced consumers to move money into nonbank financial investments with high yields, rather than into thrift institutions. The result was severe disruption of the flow of savings into thrifts and mutual savings banks. In a case study of Fed policy making, Mayer (1982) argues that this result was completely unanticipated and perceived as an embarrassing policy making failure. Regulation Q ceilings nevertheless persisted for quite some time as a basic tool to protect thrift institutions and stabilize the flow of funds into the mortgage market. Complete repeal of Regulation Q authority was recommended in a variety of financial regulatory reform acts in the 1970s and repeal of the regulation was finally accomplished with DIDMCA. The ensuing competition for funds among thrift institutions had further unanticipated results that culminated with the failure of a number of thrift institutions even before the ceilings were fully eliminated in 1986.

Persistence of Selective Controls

Margin requirements are specifically intended to slow the growth of credit to finance a particular type of economic activity. Regulation Q ceilings are specifically intended to maintain a stable flow of credit into the mortgage market. The persistence of these selective controls is puzzling given the repudiation of similar selective measures with similar enforcement mechanisms and similar goals. The economic merits and drawbacks of direct selective controls have been the subject of a modest economic literature (summarized in Hodgman 1972). Economists and central bankers agree that selective controls are not entirely effective. First, enforcement problems are inexorable and costs of administering direct controls can therefore be quite high. Second, market mechanisms are distorted by government activity. Contemporary consumers and producers would be dismayed by regulations that artificially depressed demand for consumer durables or automobiles. Finally, entrepreneurial innovation will inevitably subvert even simple controls. Money market mutual funds allowed banks to pay interest on deposits despite Regulation Q. Automobile manufacturers created sources of credit (the General Motors Acceptance Corporation) to counteract bank lending restrictions. These criticisms must certainly apply to margin requirements and interest rate ceilings. Margin requirements, for instance, have uncertain effects on market outcomes. Regulation Q ceilings can actually depress savings flows into financial institutions.

Why do these controls persist? One primary characteristic distinguishes the persistent controls from other direct controls: shared regulatory authority. Regulation Q and margin requirements are part of broader coordinated regulatory effort. The Fed implemented Regulation Q in the context of broader effort to encourage the flow of funds into mutual savings banks and thrifts supervised by other federal and state bank regulators. Opposition to Regulation Q and demands for reform appeared only when technological changes placed member banks of the Fed at a competitive disadvantage to other financial institutions (Meier 1985). Margin requirements are also part of broader set of regulations and agencies (notably, the Securities and Exchange Commission) that oversee equity markets. Opposition to margin requirements, if any, is diffused across these regulators. Margin requirements do not invite vocal opposition from a geographically widespread constituency. Margin requirements do not threaten central bank autonomy.

DIRECT SELECTIVE CONTROLS AND CENTRAL BANK AUTONOMY

During the Korean conflict, the Fed was given specific authority by the president to regulate the terms of credit for consumer installment plans (Regulation W) and home mortgages (Regulation X). Since this period the Fed has resisted the adoption of monetary policy practices that create opportunities for the influence of monetary policy outcomes by groups or individuals representing credit-sensitive economic sectors—home buyers, automobile manufacturers, and consumer finance companies. The experience of the Fed with Regulation W suggests that central bankers are reluctant to accept discretion or authority if the consequence is interference with monetary policy choices by affected interests.

Ahearn (1963) examined in detail the variety of instrumental, procedural, and technical changes undertaken inside the Fed to develop a flexible monetary policy under the terms of the Federal Reserve—Treasury Accord negotiated in 1951. From the adoption of the terms of the Accord through the mid-1960s, the Board of Governors of the Fed retreated from a variety of policy instruments—selective controls on consumer credit and residential mortgage credit, open market operations in long-term government securities, and reserve requirements on bank assets. These choices frustrated elected officials in the White House and the Congress. Each of the choices made it more difficult for elected officials to influence the distribution of monetary restraint and ease. Ahearn concludes that policy choices in the 1950s reflected too little economic theory and too many of the reservations in the Board of Governors about the political costs associated with specific policy instruments.

The model of central bank behavior described by Chant and Acheson (1986) links the choice of monetary instruments to the maintenance of central bank discretion. Central bankers choose instruments that are indirect and appear to be non-arbitrary. The Fed has adopted selective rules directly affecting the lending practices of commercial banks—discount window lending standards, differential reserve requirements, and voluntary lending campaigns. At the same, Fed decision makers adamantly opposed selective controls that directly affected the lending practices of mortgage lenders, automobile dealers, consumer finance organizations, and state and local governments. Both of the selective controls that persist after 1952 are administered in concert with other regulators, so Fed autonomy is not directly threatened by opposition to the controls. Pressure to accommodate narrow economic interests is diffused across regulators.

The procedural strategy of the central bank is clear. Rules should contain opposition to member banks and target benefits to member banks. The Board of Governors relies on indirect mechanisms that make selective restraint minimally intrusive for nonbank financial intermediaries and nonmembers of the Fed. Voluntary programs and discount window lending standards are not directly binding, so even member commercial banks have an inexpensive non-compliance alternative. The Fed can impose the costs of monetary restraint *through banks* on individual borrowers rather than imposing costs directly on banks (reserve requirements on assets) or directly upon borrowers (direct selective controls).

Chant and Acheson (1972) conclude that the Bank of Canada has distinct preferences for covert controls. Covert controls increase central bank autonomy. Covert controls are also used by the Fed to indirectly affect the flow of funds and allocate credit consistent with needs of monetary and credit policy. Much like differential reserve requirements, covert controls substitute a political process of credit allocation for market mechanisms. Covert controls, however, provide substantial discretion for central bank decision makers over the specification of the goals of allocation. Over time, decision makers in the Fed have substituted covert controls, administered through the discount window and supervisory functions, for overt controls applied directly to various borrowers. This substitution protects the Fed from the distributive conflicts that inevitably accompany decisions about money, credit, and interest rates. Members of Congress were reluctant to alter or contest these procedural choices. Administration of direct controls and extensive intervention in the Treasury market requires coordination of Fed actions with the White House and invites White House influence over monetary policy choices. For members of Congress, covert and indirect instruments were preferable to White House control. Fed autonomy challenged political control over monetary policy outcomes and frustrated White House attempts to control macroeconomic and capital market outcomes.

NOTES

1. *Annual Report of the Board of Governors of the Federal Reserve System.* 1945. Board of Governors of the Federal Reserve System: Washington D.C.

2. CEA. Quarterly Report to the President. 1 April 1947. Folder: *Quarterly Report to the President—First Quarter, 1947.* Papers of Leon Keyserling. Box #2. Harry S Truman Library.

3. Letter. Leon Keyserling to Senator Joseph O'Mahoney, Chairman of the Joint Economic Committee. 20 Nov 1950. Folder: *White House Contacts—Harry S Truman.* Papers of Leon Keyserling. Box #8. Harry S Truman Library.

4. Letter. Marriner Eccles to Governor's Councilor Patrick J. McDonough. 15 April 1947. Folder: *OF 151. (April-December, 1947)* Box #535. Official File. Papers of Harry S Truman. Harry S Truman Library.

5. Memo. Letter. Jake Vardeman to Clark Clifford. 17 October 1946. Folder: *Regulation W.* Box #12. Files of Clark Clifford. Harry S Truman Library.

6. Note. Position of the Board of Governors on Regulation W. 18 March 1947. Folder *OF 151 (1945-March,1947).* Box #635. Papers of Harry S Truman. Harry S Truman Library.

7. Letter. Truman to Eccles. 5 June 1947. Folder: *OF 151 (1945-March 1947).* Box #635. Papers of Harry S Truman. Harry S Truman Library.

8. CEA. Quarterly Report to the President. 1 April 1951. Folder: *Quarterly Report to the President—First Quarter, 1951.* Papers of Leon Keyserling. Box #2. Harry S Truman Library.

9. *Government Credit*, Hearings Before the Committee on Banking and Currency, House of Representatives. Part 2. June, 1947 [Shay 1953, 79].

10. Memo. Vardeman to Secretary Snyder. 23 Jan 1951. Folder: *Federal Reserve Banks. General. (1)* Papers of John W Snyder. Harry S Truman Library.

11. Statement. J. Vardeman. To Forrest, John G. Financial Editor, New York Times. 18 January 1951. Forwarded to John Steeleman. Folder: *OF 90. 1951.* Box #434. Official File. Papers of Harry S Truman. Harry S Truman Library.

12. Resume of Statement of William Martin. 22 July 1953. Folder: *OF-115c. Credit (1).* White House Central Files. Official Files. Box #566. Dwight D. Eisenhower Library.

13. Investigation of the Financial Condition of the United States. Hearings Before the Committee on Finance. United State Senate. 85th Congress. August, 1957.

14. Letter. Arthur Burns to Dwight Eisenhower 25 June 1956. Folder: *White House Correspondence 1956 (2).* Papers of Arthur Burns. Box #103. Dwight D. Eisenhower Library.

15. Letter. William Martin to Arthur Burns. 24 May 1957. Folder: *U. S. Government—Federal Reserve System—Board of Governors (3).* General Correspondence. Papers of Arthur Burns. Dwight D. Eisenhower Library.

16. Memo. William Rehnquist to Charles Stuart, Staff Assistant Counsel to the President. 20 November 1969. Folder: *Regulation W (Consumer Credit).* Box #B92. Papers of Arthur Burns. Gerald R. Ford Library.

17. Federal Reserve Press Release. 16 September 1974. Statement of the Federal Advisory Council. 16 September 1974.

18. Memo. ABEGS. Minutes of 5/26/55. 2 June 1955. Folder: *Interdepartmental Committees—ABEGS, 1955 (3).* Papers of Arthur Burns. Box #99. Dwight D. Eisenhower Library.

19. Letter. Memo. Saulnier to the CEA. 11 July 1955. Folder: *Fiscal and Monetary-Installment Credit, 1955-56.* Papers of Arthur Burns. Box #107. Dwight D. Eisenhower Library.

20. Letter. Arthur Burns to H.E. Cook, FDIC. Folder: *Fiscal and Monetary-Installment Credit, 1955-56.* Papers of Arthur Burns. Box #107. Dwight D. Eisenhower Library.

21. Memo. Ackley to the President. 17 August 1966. Folder: *FG 233. Federal Reserve System. EX.* Box #282. White House Central Files. Lyndon Baines Johnson Library.

22. Report of a System Committee. Reappraisal of the Federal Reserve Discount Mechanism. Volume 1. Board of Governors of the Federal Reserve System. August, 1971.

23. Federal Reserve Press Release. 19 July 1968. Folder: *Government-Federal Reserve Board: General: Federal Reserve Board 1968. (2 of 2).* Papers of Henry Fowler. Box #25E. Lyndon Baines Johnson Library.

24. *Report of a System Committee. Reappraisal of the Federal Reserve Discount Mechanism.* Volume 1. Board of Governors of the Federal Reserve System. August, 1971. (24).

25. *Annual Report of the Board of Governors of the Federal Reserve System.* 1951. Board of Governors of the Federal Reserve System: Washington, D.C.

26. Memo. Saulnier to Harold Stassen. 17 July 1959. Folder *OF-115-E. Inflation (3)*. Box #568. White House Central Files. Dwight D. Eisenhower Library.

27. Memo. William Martin to Harry S Truman. 28 September 1951. Folder: *OF-190. Bonus—World War II.* Papers of Harry Truman. Official Files. Harry S Truman Library.

28. Letter. Harry Truman to Charles Wilson. Director, Office of Defense Mobilization. 24 March 1952. Folder *OF 151 (1950)* Box #635. Official Files. Papers of Harry S Truman. Harry S Truman Library.

29. Memo. Gardner Ackley to the President. 8 March 1965. Folder: *FI. Finance.* Papers of Lyndon Baines Johnson. Confidential Files. Box #41. Lyndon Baines Johnson Library.

30. Letter. Arthur Burns to Henry Reuss. 18 Feb 1975. Folder: *Reserve Requirements, 1974.* Box #B93. Papers of Arthur Burns. Gerald R. Ford Library.

31. Memo. Martin to the President. 6 October 1965. Folder: *FI. Finance.* Box #41. Confidential Files. Paper of Lyndon Baines Johnson. Lyndon Baines Johnson Library.

32. Deposit Interest Rate Ceilings and Housing Credit. The Report of the President's Interagency Task Force on Regulation Q. Printed for the Senate Committee on the Banking, Housing, and Urban Affairs. 24 September 1979

33. Memo. Milton Semer to Lyndon Johnson. 13 September 1966. Folder: *LE/FI8.* LE Series. Box # 51. Lyndon Baines Johnson Library.

CHAPTER 6

Macroeconomic Outcomes and Monetary Policy Institutions

The monetary policy institutions described in the preceding chapters are important and variable characteristics of the domestic political process that produces monetary policy outcomes. A number of monetary policy outcomes are potentially meaningful for elected officials. Macroeconomic outcomes and capital market outcomes have motivated supervision of monetary policy choices by both the White House and the Congress. In this chapter and in Chapter 7, I identify the incentives for supervision of monetary policy created by macroeconomic and capital market outcomes. I also specify the mechanisms chosen by elected officials to influence central bank activity. Finally, I assess the efficacy of these mechanisms of control given the institutional changes observed after World War II. This chapter addresses macroeconomic outcomes. Chapter 7 describes the availability and use of alternative programs and agencies to affect capital market outcomes in the absence of central bank compliance with political goals. In both chapters I conclude that capital market objectives and distributive goals dominate macroeconomic goals in the selection of policy instruments by central bankers. In the published literature on monetary politics the incentives for political control are almost always linked to macroeconomic objectives. Institutional responses within the central bank are instead designed to control distributive conflict over monetary policy choices

Political conflict over central bank activity is associated with three types of outcomes related to monetary policy: macroeconomic performance, the distribution of monetary restraint across sectors of economy, and constraints on government finance. Each of these types of outcomes has at one time or another been the focus of observers of monetary politics. Kane (1980, 1988) concludes that the penultimate reason for the existence of Fed is the need for a macroeconomic policy scapegoat. Grier (1989) concludes that the Fed engineers monetary and macroeconomic outcomes that benefit incumbent presidents at election. Brennan and Buchanan (1981) argue that revenue constraints compel governments to rely on the central bank for inflation surprises to generate revenue in the short-term. Elected officials attempt to manipulate monetary policy instruments to achieve these political objectives. Monetary policy institutions chosen by central bankers have often frustrated these attempts. Macroeconomic outcomes and incentives for manipulating macroeconomic outcomes have been incorporated and developed in general models of the political economy. The mechanisms used to affect particular macroeconomic outcomes have received less attention, as have distributive incentives and capital market outcomes. In this chapter, I focus narrowly on the incentives for elected officials to manage macroeconomic outcomes and evaluate the extent to which postwar institutional changes have satisfied these objectives. How do monetary policy institutions abet or frustrate the manipulation of macroeconomic outcomes? Do monetary policy institutions create or reduce incentives for macroeconomic manipulation?

INCENTIVES FOR MACROECONOMIC MANIPULATION

Explanations of political activity associated with macroeconomic outcomes appeal to distinct theories about the behavior and preferences of elected officials. In order to explain the frequency and types of monitoring and action related to monetary policy, a diverse group of motivations are attributed to elected officials: cynical electoral goals, partisan redistributive goals, and collective goals (typically price stability). These goals often imply contradictory roles for the monetary authority.

Elections and the Macroeconomy

Political supervision of monetary policy is at the core of a growing literature on the link between macroeconomic policy and elections. Electoral incentives are invoked to explain cyclical variations in economic outcomes consistent with the timing of elections: political business cycles. Proponents of political business cycle theories argue that incumbent politicians manipulate economic instruments under their control in order to bring about optimal levels of economic performance immediately before elections. Some of the most empirically distinguished work on political business cycle models provides labor market micro-foundations for the real macroeconomic effects of political manipulation. Workers commit to nominally fixed wage contracts and then produce output consistent with anticipated real wages (Alesina et al 1993). Expected low inflation can produce high output. Expected high inflation results in low output. The explicit assumption is that the incumbent president controls the inflation rate and can generate inflation "surprises" after elections. Pre-election output is conditioned on low inflation rates in the future. Actual inflation rates are high, so output drops following elections (Alesina and Sachs 1988).

Nordhaus (1975) models the options facing the incumbent as a simple intertemporal maximization problem. Political actors place little value on present economic performance, but attach a premium to future outcomes near election dates. Economic planners, who share the same objective function as voters and the politicians, value present outcomes more highly than the discounted future. Political actors, to the dismay of economic planners, will engineer recessions after elections in order to enjoy prosperity near elections in the future. In another variant of the political business cycle approach, Tufte (1978) concludes that elected officials will use any instrument available in order to maximize the discretionary income of prospective voters at or near election. Transfer payments, tax rebates, and monetary stimulus should all coincide with election dates. Any of the political business cycle models would predict cyclical variation in inflation rates with high inflation immediately following elections and low inflation immediately before elections.

Inflation and Dynamic Inconsistency

Central bank activities directed at macroeconomic outcomes can relax the revenue constraint facing legislators and executives. Inflation can reduce financing constraints imposed by large debts in two ways. First, unanticipated inflation redistributes wealth from lenders to borrowers. Long-term debt contracts often specify fixed rates of interest, so unexpected inflation penalizes the lender. As the world's largest borrower the United States government would benefit from inflation. Second, purchase of public debt by the Fed "monetizes" debt. The Fed purchases government debt by crediting the reserve accounts of commercial banks that sell government securities to the System. Commercial banks can in turn use the reserve credit to make loans to customers, expanding the real level of money in the financial system. Since nearly all of the interest on government securities held by the Federal Reserve Banks is rebated to the Treasury, aggressive Fed buying can reduce the costs of debt financing.

Conservative advocates of reform of central bank practices argue that monetary policy institutions present irresistible and persistent temptations for elected officials who wish to provide services without raising taxes (Buchanan and Brennan 1981). Others argue that politicians are simply using a revenue-raising instrument that may be superior to taxes. If a government faces a choice between increasing the tax rate and increasing the inflation rate in order to meet debt financing costs, then there must be some kind of optimal point where the social costs of inflation are preferable to distortions created by further tax rate increases (Phelps 1973). Mankiw (1987) identifies this type of tradeoff in a model of U.S. tax rates and Treasury bill yields from 1952-1985. This generic temptation to generate inflation in any individual period is a problem of dynamic inconsistency: any government is better off in the long run (with respect to social welfare) by committing to a fixed inflation rate for a period of infinite duration. In any future period any government is better off deviating from the fixed path in order to enjoy a revenue windfall. The optimal strategies of the government are inconsistent over time (Kydland and Prescott 1977).

In practice, every member of Congress and every president benefits from unanticipated inflation to relax government financing constraints in the short-term (more spending at no cost). Woolley (1985) and others conclude that persistent demands for inflation are the root cause of inflation in the postwar United States economy. Cyclical models of economic outcomes (notably the political business cycle models described above) fail to recognize the gains to government from persistent and high rate of expansion of the monetary base (White 1988). McClure and Willett (1988) conclude that the U.S. government realized substantial revenue gains from the inflation surges in the late 1960s and early 1970s when actual inflation greatly exceeded anticipated inflation. The government incurred costs when actual inflation was below expected inflation in the early 1980s. Models of oversight and bank behavior that are informed by the dynamic inconsistency perspective would predict persistent and high inflation (at least until the distortions introduced by new taxes are lower than the distortions introduced by further acceleration in inflation).

Political Parties and the Inflation Rate

Hibbs (1987) identifies distinctive partisan strategies for management of the macroeconomy. The Democratic party relies on the support of blue-collar workers and middle to low income families that are vulnerable to economic dislocation from unemployment. Republican constituents are more likely to be wealthy and therefore inflation-averse. Confronted with a trade-off between inflation and unemployment, Democrats are more likely to tolerate inflation and Republicans are more likely to tolerate unemployment. Alesina and Rosenthal (1995) develop a rational expectations variant of the partisan business cycle model, predicting transient shocks in real economic variables from changes in the partisan identity of the president. Like the sophisticated political business cycle models, the incumbent is assumed to have control over the rate of inflation. Changing partisan control of the White House produces variation in the inflation rate (although the effects are somewhat attenuated by shared control of Congress). Chappell, Havrilesky & McGregor (1993) identify distinctive behavior by members of the Board of Governors appointed by Democratic and Republican presidents between 1960 and 1987. Democratic appointees are more likely than Republican appointees to favor monetary ease (and risk higher inflation). Overall, we should expect to observe fairly stable levels of inflation, punctuated by declines under Republican administrations and increases in Democratic administrations. Changes in the inflation rate should be abrupt if presidential influence is direct and precise. Changes should be very gradual if the appointment process is the mechanism for affecting monetary policy choices.

Delegation and Benefits of Price Stability

Rogoff (1985) and Alesina and Gatti (1995) describe the central bank as a commitment device. Legislators create and tolerate autonomous central banks to enjoy the collective benefit of price stability. Appointment of conservative or inflation-averse central bankers results in long run stability of the price level. The inflation experience of the United States in the 1990s and the inflation experience of Germany and the *Bundesbank* are typically cited as evidence of successful delegation and restraint. Central bank independence is increasingly described in more theoretical work as highly desirable for economic stability and output (Fisher 1995, MacCallum 1995).

By delegating monetary policy to a conservative central bank, legislators manage to solve a collective action problem. Delegation delivers price stability despite electoral and partisan temptations introduced by inflation surprises. Krehbiel (1991) describes how members of Congress use committees to overcome problems of information in a way that benefits Congress collectively. An autonomous Fed may deliver benefits that are similarly collective. Central bank autonomy forecloses allocation of capital to privileged constituents or groups. The puzzle is how these types of commitment devices or collective goods emerge (Knight, 1992). Why are collectively beneficial institutions proposed or accepted by members who must act contrary to self-interest in the creation and maintenance of the institutions? An autonomous Fed makes it difficult to achieve partisan or electoral goals with monetary policy. Which members of what Congress endorsed this monetary arrangement? Descriptions of delegation and commitment of monetary authority focus on the effects and not the origins of decisions to delegate (Rogoff 1985, Alesina and Gatti 1995). Questions of origin and maintenance are generally not addressed, so the conditions under which commitment devices may be altered or undone is unclear. Models of commitment and delegation would consistently predict low levels and low variability of inflation. The inflation experience in the United States does not suggest that commitment to price stability has been remarkably binding, although recent low levels of inflation have reinforced the idea that autonomy may produce desirable long-term outcomes. If delegation if effective, then inflation should be consistently low.

Why Incentives Fail to Explain Outcomes

Empirical analysis of macroeconomic policy outcomes has failed to point to a specific motivation for elected officials that can predict particular central bank actions—a weakness of the scholarship on monetary policy. For example, under what conditions should a central bank be expected to generate low inflation (a public good), generate high inflation (meet short-term revenue needs), or generate variable inflation timed to coincide with electoral goals? Is there one explanation that can accommodate the policy failures of the 1970s and policy successes of the 1990s?

The likelihood of observing each outcome certainly depends on the institutional context that translates preferences of elected officials into policy outcomes. In this case, the formal rules (the Federal Reserve Act, for instance) are insufficiently descriptive of the institutional context. The Federal Reserve Act was not updated substantially between the period of relatively high inflation in the 1970s and relatively low inflation in the 1990s. The most important formal changes, reporting requirements imposed on the Fed after 1978 under Humphrey-Hawkins, would be expected to lead to more variability in inflation as the demands of elected officials are transmitted to the Fed. This has not been the case. Each of the political economy approaches finds some outcomes data to support expectations about either monetary growth or levels of inflation. The data do not permit identification of a single motivation that dominates the decisions of elected officials about monetary policy delegation and monitoring. There are at least two explanations for this poor link between incentives and outcomes: insufficient opportunity to influence the central bank (no mechanism of control) or insufficient technical control over outcomes within the central bank (weak transmission mechanism for monetary policy).

OPPORTUNITIES TO INFLUENCE MONETARY POLICY

Cyclical variation in economic outcomes like inflation could be induced by changes in any of the instruments of monetary policy: the discount rate, open market operations, reserve requirements, selective controls or moral suasion. Members of Congress rarely provide any explicit direction for the Fed to update any of these instruments. Members of Congress have developed formal rules for Fed reporting and disclosure of monetary policy targets and choices, but these rules require no specific information about implementation at the level of instruments. The White House is much more likely to provide specific instructions for coordinated changes in Fed instruments: specific requests for open market purchases or changes in the discount rate. White House influence is typically informal, but, by most accounts, the informal influence of the president is more effective than the formal channels created by members of Congress.

Coordination and Executive Influence

Coordination of executive actions and central bank policy has conventionally been quite informal. Before 1957, the president either discussed policy goals with a recent appointment to the Board of Governors, transmitted requests for accommodation through the Secretary of the Treasury or the CEA, or (less frequently) corresponded directly with the Chairman of the Board of Governors of the Federal Reserve System. For instance, Dwight Eisenhower relied on Secretary of the Treasury Humphrey to "put the utmost pressure" on Chairman William Martin to supply bank reserves and ease credit in April, 1954.[1]

Staff at the White House later initiated regular informal meetings between the Chairman of the CEA, the Director of the Bureau of the Budget, the Secretary of the Treasury, the Chairman of the Board of Governors of the Federal Reserve System, and the president. This small group—designated the *Quadriad* during the Kennedy Administration—was designed to include the Fed in the policy making deliberations of the executive branch.[2] In practice, the extent of the coordination was limited, especially when sensitive issues were discussed. Before a Quadriad meeting to discuss the 1967 Budget Outlook, the Director of the Bureau of the Budget cautioned Lyndon Johnson:

> In a meeting at which Bill Martin is present I would recommend that we not discuss the Defense expenditure forecast. This might simply push him towards a tighter money policy.[3]

In addition to the regular Quadriad meetings, monetary policy has been supervised directly by a few presidents. Frequent direct meetings between Arthur Burns and the president were the most important source of coordination in the mid-1970s (Kettl 1986).

Substantively, the president exerts the most effort in each of these contexts to dissuade members of the Board of Governors from raising the discount rate—the lending rate for reserves borrowed from the regional Reserve Banks. In April 1956, the White House attempted to directly persuade William Martin to postpone an increase in the discount rate.[4] The discount rate was nevertheless increased twice in 1956 from 2 percent to 2.5 percent and then to 3 percent before the November elections. Throughout his term,. Lyndon Johnson received detailed political intelligence about the probable voting patters of the Board of Governors. He knew the expected votes of each member of the Board of Governors and solicited information that could change the votes of particular Board members. He was particularly interested (and unsuccessful) in averting a discount rate increase in late 1965.[5] White House staff typically appraise the president of changes in key monetary aggregates and recent Fed open market activity, but direct presidential attention is more likely when the Board of Governors anticipates changes in the discount rate.

Oversight and Congressional Influence

After the creation of the Joint Committee on the Economic Report in the Employment Act of 1946, members of Congress conducted occasional and infrequent hearings to assess the conduct of monetary policy by the Fed. Two subcommittees of the Joint Committee on the Economic Report addressed the relationship between the executive branch and the central bank during the Truman Administration. The Douglas Committee reaffirmed the independence of the central bank; the Patman Committee questioned the subordination of executive authority to independent agencies. This occasional oversight, typically directed toward the structure of decision making and the influence of the White House, was replaced by a substantive and permanent oversight mechanism in the mid-1970s. Designated House Concurrent Resolution 133 (HCR 133), this set of rules compelled the Board of Governors of the Federal Reserve System to specify targets for the growth rate of the various monetary aggregates. The rules contained no mandate to specify targets for ultimate macroeconomic objectives.

Observers of monetary policy oversight in the United State Congress have been unable to agree upon the scope and efficacy of oversight when directed specifically at control of the monetary aggregates. Grier (1991) concludes that congressional oversight matters. Changes in rollcall voting scores of the Senate Banking Committee (as reported by Americans for Democratic Action) help to predict the rate of growth of the narrow money aggregate—M1. Havrilesky (1988) concludes that congressional oversight does not matter. His index of congressional statements on monetary policy abstracted from the Wall Street Journal fails to predict changes in the growth rate of the narrow money aggregate.

Besides occasional oversight and HCR 133, several informal committees have emerged as to castigate the Fed when interest rates reached historic highs, only to disappear as interest rates stabilized. Wright Patman, for instance, established an unofficial steering committee in opposition to high interest rates in December, 1967.[6] These ad hoc committees do not specify macroeconomic objectives to guide Fed conduct of monetary policy, but are instead vehicles for constituent demands for redistribution of the burdens of monetary restraint.[7] It is unclear how members of the Board of Governors respond to these demands. There is no institutionalized channel for the transmission of these distributive demands from members of Congress to the Board of Governors of the Federal Reserve System. Existing work has identified a number of monetary policy outputs that can be used to evaluate the relative influence of members of Congress and the President over monetary outcomes. The empirical results are far from conclusive.

EVIDENCE OF INFLUENCE FROM OUTCOMES AND TARGETS

Technical Uncertainty

In the introduction to this work I described a robust consensus that has in recent years informed general models of the political economy: the president is the decisive actor in the political process that produces monetary policy outcomes. This conclusion is somewhat surprising given our limited knowledge about the link between policy choices and ultimate macroeconomic outcomes. Unfortunately, the link between changes in the instruments of monetary policy and ultimate objectives is ambiguous and variable over time. The exact structural relationship is both unknown and the subject of controversy among macroeconomists (Bernanke and Blinder 1992, Sims 1980). This uncertainty is rarely reflected in models of the political economy. Recent work on political business cycle models, for instance, assumes that incumbent presidents simply have direct control over macroeconomic outcomes like the inflation rate (Alesina et al 1993). The objective mechanism of control is left unspecified.

Other Sources of Uncertainty

The types of goals or objectives that are assigned to monetary policy by various presidents varies considerably over time. Empirical confirmation of the competing theories of macroeconomic manipulation is evasive since the range of instruments and indicators of performance used by economic policy makers are updated frequently. The Ford White House staff closely monitored targets and growth paths for the monetary aggregates. Much earlier, the CEA under Harry S Truman could not have tracked growth in any of the various monetary aggregates. The only indicators of monetary policy used within the government were money market conditions: interest rates and bank reserves. Public statements and internal deliberations reveal that the discount rate, not the monetary aggregates, were monitored closely by the White House under Eisenhower and Johnson.

The diversity of goals and indicators does not imply that important electoral goals are not wedded to central bank activity. Under President Truman important election year commitments were made concerning the maintenance of prices in the market for government bonds. One component of the Accord between the Treasury and the Fed was purported to be a maintenance of the price level of government bonds until after the 1952 election. As evidence of performance, the discount rate was stable from the announcement of the Treasury Accord until just after the election in 1952. Executive influence to maintain the discount rate was also intended to prevent monetary restraint during the 1956 Presidential election and the midterm elections of 1966. The net effect of these attempts is still unclear, even with considerable retrospection.

The election of 1960 led to bitter criticism of the Fed from Republican candidate Richard Nixon. According to some accounts, Nixon attributed his 1960 defeat to the monetary policy choices of the

Fed (Stein, 1994). Ironically, the Fed had no intention of implementing monetary restraint during the election year. In fact, immediately before the election both Treasury staff and the Fed anticipated considerable monetary ease during the fall campaign:

> The cumulative effect of all this action will be 605 million dollars and possible credit expansion of 3.5 billion dollars. It is being timed to meet seasonal needs of the economy in September, but is designed to put money into the System in excess of seasonal needs.[8]

Retrospective assessments of Fed action in 1960 led observers in the Johnson Administration to anticipate untimely Fed restraint near the 1964 election. Seymour Harris, Senior Consultant to the Treasury, warned Johnson of the electoral liabilities of monetary restraint:

> In 1956 and 1959-60, restrictive monetary policies and very large increases in the rate of interest occurred. In 1956, this did not matter, for Eisenhower had a large lead. But it was very costly to the Nixon candidacy, for it greatly increased unemployment. In 1964, it is *imperative* that the government exclude a restrictive monetary policy.[9]

It is unclear what types of instruments or outcomes were monitored by these observers reporting either excessive ease or unwarranted restraint. Fed and Treasury actors believed that they were increasing monetary reserves during the election season. The poor economic performance and low money growth rates were unanticipated.

Cargill (1989) argues that the formal independence of the United States central bank requires indirect communication of political demands through channels and actors that vary over time. Central bank compliance with these demands is therefore difficult to predict. In each postwar administration a different variable was the focus of White House attention and a different action was required by the Fed to satisfy White House demands. Truman focused on bond prices. Eisenhower monitored the discount rate. Systematic evidence of manipulation involving one instrument or another across a several elections or administrations would be not only fortuitous, but misleading.

Evaluating the Scope of Influence

Each of the incentives for macroeconomic intervention (electoral, partisan, fiscal) has a straightforward empirical implication. The link between elections and the macroeconomy should be particularly unambiguous. Economic outcomes should improve preceding elections; outcomes should deteriorate after elections. Researchers investigating this link typically evaluate economic performance by measuring the growth rate (or change in the growth rate) of three macroeconomic indicators: the Gross National Product, the rate of unemployment, and the inflation rate. Beck (1990(a)) tests for a cyclical component in the variation over time in unemployment—he fails to confirm the existence of a political business cycle. Haynes and Stone (1988) find cyclical variation consistent with political business cycles in both inflation and unemployment. The macroeconomic evidence is, unfortunately, ambiguous.

The failure to observe outcomes consistent with the political business cycle could be a function of technical uncertainty (Fed actions do not produce intended outcomes) or the dominance of other incentives (partisan or revenue-generating goals). If technical uncertainty explains the absence of a political business cycle, then monetary policy choices and targets may independently exhibit cycles consistent with change near elections. Open market purchases may accelerate before elections and decelerate immediately after elections. Cyclical variation in the broader monetary aggregates would be also expected if the Fed were an active participant in the production of political business cycles.

Evidence from Monetary Aggregates

The focus of much empirical work on the Fed and the politics of monetary policy has been confined to a narrow set of policy indicators that measure the aggregate tightness or ease of monetary policy. These policy indicators—the growth rate of the narrow money aggregate (M1), changes in the federal funds rate or the discount rate, and variation in excess bank reserves—are chosen as measures of monetary policy outcomes since they are to some extent controlled by the Fed. Changes in ultimate macroeconomic objectives are much more difficult to attribute exclusively to Fed choices. Research on central bank compliance with executive demands has relied on two of these indicators to measure the extent of presidential control: the federal funds rate and the narrow money aggregate (M1). The data at the level of instruments simply do not support the conclusion that presidents control monetary policy outcomes.

In 1978 a staff member of the House Subcommitee on Domestic Monetary Policy, Robert Weintraub, proposed a measure of monetary restraint that could be used to capture the extent to which presidential preferences are reflected in the growth rates of the monetary aggregates. Changes in the growth rate of narrow money aggregate was linked by Weintraub to distinctive administration monetary policy preferences. He concluded that "in each administration monetary policy fitted harmoniously with the President's economic and financial objectives and plans." (Weintraub 1978, 350) The Weintraub data are reproduced in Table 1.

The Weintraub data and conclusions have been cited many times in the literature on monetary politics. The Social Science Citation Index records 35 citations of the 1978 piece in the last ten years. This is a relatively large number of citations given the narrow published literature on the politics of monetary policy. The conclusions that Weintraub drew from the aggregate data have the been the basis of further research on the timing of changes in the monetary aggregates. A particular emphasis has been on estimating the relationship between the growth rate of the narrow money aggregate and the timing of elections.[12] The results are ambiguous. Beck (1987) concludes that the proximity of elections does not explain the growth rate of monetary aggregates if appropriate controls for fiscal policy are included. Grier (1989) insists that a small yet statistically significant part of money supply growth can be explained by the timing of elections.[13] In a more general evaluation of the link between administration objectives and money growth rates, Havrilesky (1988) showed that administration signaling—as communicated in the Wall Street Journal—has a significant impact on the direction of monetary policy as reflected in the money aggregates.

Table 1
Monetary policy thrust in each president's term, 1951-1977 (Weintraub, 1978)

President	Years.	M1 Money Supply Measure[10]	M1 Measure Adjusted for Unemployment[11]
Truman.	1951-1952.	4.75	0.81
Eisenhower.	1953-1960.	1.73	-2.30
Kennedy.	1961-1963.	2.31	-1.78
Johnson.	1964-1968.	4.78	0.82
Nixon.	1969-1973.	6.17	2.18
Ford.	1974-1976.	4.76	0.61
Carter.	1977 Only.	6.61	2.50

Source: Weintraub (1978)

After 1980 the stable empirical relationship that had characterized the relationship between the narrow money aggregate (M1) and economic performance (reflected in GNP) began to change. Sharp and unexpected changes in the velocity of M1 (the ratio of the nominal GNP to the money aggregate) frustrated precise targeting of aggregates for the purpose of controlling economic growth rates. As a result, M1 was no longer treated as an independently reliable indicator of Fed monetary policy activity. M2—a broader money aggregate—and a number of other broader and different aggregates (divisia aggregates, for instance) have been suggested as substitutes. The Weintraub measures and a broader measure based on M2 are reproduced with current data in Table 2.

Table 2
Monetary policy thrust in each president's term, 1959-1996

President	Years.	M1 Money Supply Measure	M1 Measure Adjusted for Unemployment	M2 Money Supply Measure[14]
Eisenhower.	1959 1960.	0.99	-2.91	4.85
Kennedy.	1961-1963.	2.81	-1.29	7.70
Johnson.	1964-1968.	5.08	1.08	7.24
Nixon.	1969-1973.	5.54	1.56	7.96
Ford.	1974-1976.	5.84	1.75	11.72
Carter.	1977-1980.	7.27	3.21	8.04
Reagan I.	1981-1984.	7.59	3.40	9.29
Reagan II.	1985-1988.	8.13	4.05	5.95
Bush.	1989-1992.	7.09	3.07	3.22
Clinton	1993-1996.	0.88	-3.17	3.08

Source: Federal Reserve Economic Database. Federal Reserve Bank of St. Louis

On the basis of either money aggregate, the money growth rate under Republican presidents is higher than under Democrats. Bill Clinton and Dwight Eisenhower appear to share the same preferences over money growth rates. This is a curious finding, given the conventional assumption that Democrats are more likely than Republicans to resist anti-inflation measures (Hargrove and Morley 1987, Hibbs 1987). Besides appealing to uncontrollable exogenous events, the high money growth rate could have one of two explanations in the context of the incentives described above. It could be the case that monetary aggregates simply do not reflect executive preferences. It could also be the case that the aversion of Republican presidents to high taxes compels expansion of the money supply to raise revenue. Neither explanation is consist with the assumptions of political business cycle theories or partisan theories of central bank behavior. In short, the aggregates are highly uninformative about what kinds of incentives drive oversight or how elected officials obtain central bank compliance with macroeconomic demands.

Evidence from the Federal Funds Rate

Beck (1987) explicitly links variation in the federal funds rate to changes in the identity of the president. Changes in this interest rate—a policy target for the Fed for much of the postwar period—can indicate a change in the direction of monetary policy. Beck concludes that movement in this indicator of Fed activity fails to support political business cycle hypotheses. It is difficult, however, to evaluate theories of political influence with the federal funds rate. The link between movement of the federal funds rate and macroeconomic outcomes is ambiguous. First, during periods of monetary restraint commercial bank demands for funds can be satisfied by discount window borrowing. The funds rate can remain deceptively high relative to the price of funds for other money market instruments. An important source of downward variation in the funds rate is suppressed by the availability of discount window loans. Second, the federal funds rate may remain stable when required reserves are increased or decreased, since open market operations offset the immediate market shocks of reserve adjustments. The lag between policy action and funds rate movements may either disguise or exaggerate cyclical variation in monetary instruments.

Evidence from Direct Policy Instruments

Institutional changes within the Fed could facilitate compliance with macroeconomic demands. The rehabilitation of discount window lending as an instrument of monetary policy after 1968 is consistent with the informal coordination of White House objectives with central bank policy. Since discount window lending criteria may be modified by the central bank to influence commercial bank lending practices, the discount window could be an effective variable instrument and an important component of efforts to vary the inflation rate over the course of a presidential term. The use of discount window lending restrictions is practically limited, since discount window lending regulations apply only to member banks. The effectiveness of variation in lending criteria would have been limited before the 1980 passage of DIDMCA.

Persistent cyclical variation in open market operations, reserve requirements, or the level of the discount rate would be much more effective than window lending criteria for inducing cyclical variation in inflation. But both the discount rate and reserve requirements are far too static to affect macroeconomic outcomes in any precise way. Reserve requirements and the discount rates change very infrequently and almost never change during election years. Furthermore, changes in both instruments are unambiguously counter-cyclical. Discount rate changes and reserve requirement adjustments slow growth and stimulate recovery, rather than boosting a growing economy during an election or restraining a contracting economy after an election. If evidence of influence is to be evaluated using instruments, open market operations must be the primary source of variation in monetary policy that produces macroeconomic cycles or changes consistent with the incentives described above.

Open market transactions data do not provide any support for election year manipulation. In the July 1974 issue of *Fortune* magazine, Sanford Rose specifically implicated Arthur Burns in a Nixon Administration attempt to improve economic conditions immediately preceding the 1972 election. In fact, quarterly net open market purchases were negative (indicating monetary restraint) for the first and third quarters in 1972. Open market operations were high and positive in each quarter of 1971 and each quarter of 1973.[15] Either Burns was ineffective in persuading the FOMC to act favorably on the Nixon request for financial market intervention, or his overtures to the FOMC were exaggerated. Evidence of distinctly partisan patterns in open market activity is likewise weak. The most restrictive patterns of open market activity occurred under a Republican President (Eisenhower and Bills Only). The most liberal patterns of open market activity also occurred under a Republican President (Nixon and purchase of agency issues). There is simply no evidence at the level of instruments to identify one set of incentives for macroeconomic manipulation as critically important or persistent explanations for monetary policy choices.

CONCLUSION

Evidence either for or against political control of monetary policy outcomes at the level of instruments is ambiguous. The Weintraub article, probably the most frequently cited piece in the narrow literature on monetary politics, points us to data that do not support the empirical claims of most models of the political economy. Further, mechanisms used by the president and his staff to manipulate macroeconomic outcomes are ad hoc and informal. The Congress maintains a permanent oversight mechanism (a formal channel of control) but nevertheless has difficulty compelling central bank action directly. Finally, the rules used to conduct monetary policy appear to be designed more to frustrate than to abet the manipulation of macroeconomic outcomes for political gain. Overall, the persistent search for evidence of macroeconomic manipulation engineered with the complicity of the Fed has not provided many insights into the behavior and policy choices of central bankers or elected officials.

Mebane (1994) has demonstrated that elected officials use fiscal policy instruments (specifically, cuts in payroll taxes) to attempt to bring about increases in income before elections. Tufte (1978) also integrates transfer payments into the political business cycle literature. If election year monetary policy does not actively counteract this election year fiscal stimulus, then the central bank accommodates acceleration of growth or deflation brought about by changes in other instruments of macroeconomic policy. Beck (1984) suggests that this mechanism may explain some weak macroeconomic cycles. Fiscal variables, rather than electoral variables, may explain variation in the monetary instruments and indicators. If these authors are correct, then partisan and electoral incentives related to macroeconomic outcomes should be a subtext of the annual debate over tax and expenditures that takes place in the Congress. This is rarely the case.

It is most often the case that fiscal policy conflicts—whether during an election year or during off years—are dominated by distributive claims. Elected officials are advertising and attending to the needs of constituents or groups. The aggregate size of the budget or the operating deficit is typically neglected, despite incentives for manipulating deficits to affect changes in macroeconomic outcomes. This is especially the case prior to the Budget and Impoundment Control Act of 1974 (Schick 1980).

Monetary policy is often presumed to be immune from these distributive claims. Havrilesky (1988) concludes that while fiscal policy may have redistributive or macroeconomic stabilization effects, monetary policy effects are linked unambiguously to macroeconomic stabilization objectives. He then explains monetary surprises before elections as a (passive) corollary to fiscal redistribution. Distributive effects of monetary exuberance are distinctly omitted.

Monetary policy institutions and monetary policy outcomes defy a macroeconomic interpretation of American monetary politics. Distributive conflicts explain the termination and adoption of a variety of instruments that are used to conduct monetary policy. One reason why monetary politics is so confusing at times is because the rules used to conduct money and credit policies are the product of the same distributive conflicts that generate fiscal policy rules. Distributive goals dominate macroeconomic incentives in the specification and assessment of central bank rules. The macroeconomic incentives and institutional responses described in this chapter fail to provide a clear answer to the questions that are outlined in the first section of the book: Can a central banker create rules and incentives that generate central bank autonomy? How do central bank institutions condition the supervision of elected officials? Macroeconomic incentives do not reveal the full extent of the political conflict and political activity that are associated with monetary policy outcomes.

Evidence of macroeconomic manipulation—either at the level of outcomes or instruments—is weak because the content of monetary policy outcomes, like fiscal policy outcomes, is both distributive and macroeconomic. Both members of Congress and presidents desire to exercise control over the distributive characteristics of monetary policy. Decision makers in the Fed use monetary policy institutions to resist these distributive demands. The constraints on the president and the Congress that affect macroeconomic manipulations are simply residuals of this distributive conflict. The persistent and inconsistent incentives for macroeconomic manipulation are not reflected in macroeconomic outcomes. Central banking practices, typically indirect and technically imprecise, foreclose direct control over the allocation and the aggregate level of capital consistent with precise management of the macroeconomy.

NOTES

1. Diary Annotation. 8 April 1954. Folder: *DDE Personal Diary. January-November, 1954 (2).* Box #4 DDE Diary Series. Ann Whitman File. Dwight D. Eisenhower Library.

2. Draft Press Release (or Briefing Notes) for issuance when the President meets with the "Quadriad" (Dillon-Martin-Gordon-Heller). 5 January 1964. Folder: *FG 233. Federal Reserve System (EX).* Box #282. White House Central Files. Lyndon Baines Johnson Library

3. Memo. Schultze, Director, Bureau of the Budget, to The President. 31 May 1966. Folder: *FI. Finance.* Box #41 Confidential Files. Papers of Lyndon Baines Johnson. Lyndon Baines Johnson Library.

4. Telephone Calls. 12 April 1956. Folder: *April 1956 Phone Calls.* Box #15. DDE Diary Series. Ann Whitman File. Dwight D. Eisenhower Library.

5. Cable. Califano to The President. Text of Urgent Memo from Gardner Ackley to Johnson. 29 November 1965. Folder: *FG 233. Federal Reserve System (EX).* Box #282. White House Central Files. Lyndon Baines Johnson Library

6. *Congressional Record.* Proceedings and Debates of the 90th Congress. First Session. Volume 113-Part 25. Washington D.C.: United States Government. (34767-34768)

7. Congressional responses to these demands are discussed in Chapter 7, below.

8. Memo. Robert Anderson to the President. (Dictated to Ann Whitman). 8 August 1960. Folder: *ACW Diary August 1960 (2).* Box #15. Ann Whitman Diary Series. Dwight D. Eisenhower Library.

9. Memo. Seymour E. Harris, Senior Consultant to the Treasury, to the President. 4 December 1963. Folder: *FI. Finance.* Papers of Lyndon Baines Johnson. Confidential Files. Box #41. Lyndon Baines Johnson Library.

10. The money supply measure reported by Weintraub (1978) is the monthly percent change at an annual rate in the narrow money aggregate (M1), seasonally adjusted, averaged over the calendar year. Table 1 reproduces the table in Weintraub (1978, 351).

11. The adjusted money supply measure is the simple money supply measure adjusted for the prevailing rate of unemployment and growth over time in the rate of full employment. The measure is designated as Thrust 3 in Weintraub (1978). Weintraub assumes that the rate of full employment increases from 4.0 percent in 1959 to 5.5 percent in 1978. I assume that the rate of full employment remains at 5.5 percent thereafter. See Weintraub (1978) for specification and details.

12. Keech (1986) reviews much of the empirical work in a systematic assessment of political business cycles.

13. Grier (1989) and Beck (1987) test electoral cycles of various shapes by including cyclical variables in an ARIMA model of the growth path of the narrow money aggregate. They produce conflicting results.

14. The alternative money supply measure is the monthly percent change at an annual rate in the broader money aggregate (M2), seasonally

adjusted, averaged over the calendar year. Data for Table 2 are from the Federal Reserve Economic Database maintained by the Federal Reserve Bank of St. Louis.

15. Quarterly open market activity is reported in the financial market flow of funds distributed by the Federal Reserve System. See Figure 4 and related notes in Chapter 4 for information on the flow of funds and data on aggregate open market activity.

CHAPTER 7

Capital Market Flows and Federal Credit Institutions

It is clear that elected officials are highly constrained by monetary policy institutions. The absence of direct control over instruments and outcomes is the result of a mix of formal and informal constraints self-imposed by Congress and generated by the central bank. Both precise macroeconomic manipulation and direct control over the allocation of capital are foreclosed by central bank autonomy. Innovations in federal credit institutions outside of the control of the central bank have nevertheless permitted elected officials to direct capital to fairly specific classes of borrowers. Federal credit programs satisfy demands for credit from a number of categories of borrowers and enable elected officials to fulfill a number of objectives. Federal credit subsidies and guarantees partially insulate the home-building industry from cyclical fluctuations in the supply of credit, preserve bank credit to meet the demands of small business enterprise, make bank credit available for state and municipal governments, and maintain the price of government securities. Since investigation of the politics of monetary policy typically focuses on macroeconomic outcomes, the broader set of capital market outcomes are overlooked. These distributive outcomes motivate government intervention in capital markets and oversight of monetary policy choices. Monetary policy institutions have only created weak obstacles for elected officials to influence distributive outcomes.

The Fed does not provide the types of particular control over the flow of capital that members of Congress prefer. An extraordinary volume of capital is therefore allocated using other government agencies or government-sponsored financial institutions. Since the end of World War II, these federal credit programs have experienced remarkable growth in both number and size. The proliferation of credit subsidies should not occur if the Fed was subject to effective and latent control of legislators. Fed choices over instruments should ultimately produce outcomes consistent with the distributive preferences of Congress. If the Fed was anticipating the preferences of members of Congress, then the central bank would indirectly satisfy the types of distributive objectives that are currently met with federal credit programs.

Federal credit programs would expand if members of Congress tolerated Fed autonomy from the executive. Federal credit programs are simply new tools created to bring about preferred capital market outcomes in the face of central bank autonomy. Neither members of Congress nor the central bank accept (or seek) the function of reconciling competing claims for credit. There is no centralized or systematic allocation of capital across capital and money markets. Members of Congress respond to incentives for the allocation of capital across borrowers by creating a variety of discrete programs to intervene in capital markets. These programs protect some sectors and, by implication, impose costs on other sectors of the economy. The ultimate effects of this piecemeal strategy on both management of federal finances and real distribution of economic resources are unclear, but federal credit programs remain an extremely persistent and integral feature of government intervention in the financial sector of the American economy

INCENTIVES FOR THE DISTRIBUTION OF CAPITAL

The Conventional Story

There is often a rigid distinction made between policy outcomes that offer direct benefits to particular groups and policy outcomes that are universal. This distinction has been used to explain the allocation of legislative time and energy across pork barreling or national lawmaking (Fiorina 1989) and to distinguish between redistributive or distributive policy domains (Lowi 1964). Conventional accounts suggest that policies with universal outcomes will be the focus of presidential time and energy; policies with concentrated benefits will be the focus of congressional activity (Spitzer 1983).

Scholarship on monetary policy implicitly assumes that monetary policy outcomes are ultimately reflected in macroeconomic and monetary aggregates and therefore congressional interest in these outcomes is relatively low. Observers of Congress who believe oversight of the Fed is ineffective explain their findings by appealing to conventional descriptions of legislative behavior that emphasize disincentives for law-making that produces essentially collective benefits. Havrilesky (1988) summarizes:

> The vote-producing benefits from a congressperson's involvement in monetary policy are typically minor compared to alternative, pork-barrelling, activities. (Havrilesky 1988, 322)

Identifying the "Domestic Sources of American Monetary Policy," Beck (1984) focuses upon the extent to which the identity and political party of the president affect various measures of monetary policy outcomes. Although Beck considers possible influences of members of Congress on monetary policy choices, his empirical models of Fed behavior completely omit the impact of the preferences and behavior of members of Congress. The primary outcome produced by monetary policy, price stability, is a universal and collective benefit. Members of Congress are relatively unconcerned with monetary policy outcomes.

Why the Conventional Story is Insufficient

If conventional descriptions of executive supervision and legislative oversight were accurate, then the process of monetary policy oversight should follow a distinctive and persistent pattern. As prices begin to increase and evidence of inflation is publicized, presidents (independent of party) should exhort the Fed to take measures consistent with price stability. When the Fed responds, then Congress should demand (with unanimity) that the burdens of monetary restraint be lifted from particular economic sectors. This pattern does not describe American monetary politics. Three specific sets of actions by elected officials confound the conventional interpretation.

First, explicit direction from Congress to the Fed has historically divided along partisan lines. Oversight documents prepared by the Joint Economic Committee typically contain minority reports that modify instructions to the Fed: Republican and Democratic members of Congress have distinctive preferences over monetary policy choices. More overtly, in one of the few roll call votes on executive direction of monetary policy, House Democrats failed to pass legislation authorizing a Commission on Monetary and Financial Policy in the late 1950s. The Eisenhower Administration was undertaking an identical study at the same time. House Republicans uniformly supported Eisenhower. The absence of unanimity and the presence of partisan conflict are inconsistent with the expectation of conflict between executive and Congress that the conventional interpretations would suggest.

Second, both Democratic and Republican presidents have generated short-term pressure on the Fed to lower interest rates. Presidents may publicly support monetary restraint to reduce inflation, but at the same time both Republican and Democratic presidents have privately attempted to persuade members of the Board of Governors to refrain from direct actions that would actually reduce inflation in the future, particularly through changes in the discount rate. Movements in monetary aggregates (described in Chapter 6) belie either overt or hidden action by presidents to consistently reduce inflation rates and achieve price stability.

Finally, both presidents and members of Congress have advocated redistribution of the burdens of restraint away from particular economic sectors. Redistribution has been tied directly to central bank operations using open market operations, reserve requirements on assets, or direct selective controls. Redistribution has also been a feature of federal credit programs. The persistence and growth of the Small Business Administration, the Student Loan Marketing Association, the Federal National Mortgage Association, and a host of other credit providers are evidence that elected officials are sincere proponents of capital market intervention to protect particular types of borrowers. Demands for selective intervention come from the White House and from Congress.

The simple distinction between universal and particularistic benefits fails to explain conflict over monetary policy and over the allocation of credit and capital. A variety of incentives explain choices of elected officials about the pursuit of price stability: Chapter 6 outlined the electoral, partisan, and fiscal incentives for manipulation of the inflation rate. Similarly, a complex set of incentives explains choices of elected officials about intervention to distribute credit and capital. Federal credit programs can satisfy electoral, partisan, and fiscal goals. Federal credit programs can be used to channel credit to particular types of borrowers near elections. Federal credit programs can be used to reward particular constituencies that support Democrats or Republicans. Federal credit programs can provide a subsidy or resource that is difficult to subject to strict budgetary accounting. Both members of Congress and presidents have a stake in these outcomes. The conventional distinction between universal and particularistic policy outcomes artificially segregates monetary policy and federal credit programs. Monetary policy and federal credit policy are instead directly related. Institutional choices about monetary policy affect the scope and variety of federal credit programs. The scope of federal credit programs affects monetary control strategies. Members of Congress at least implicitly balance the benefits of central bank autonomy with the costs of federal credit programs (and the costs of central bank autonomy with the benefits of federal credit programs). Only rarely is the role of central bank in the allocation of capital directly addressed by Congress.

Distribution of Credit and Capital

Monetary policy choices produce distinct distributive consequences that are relevant to members of Congress. If members of Congress are strictly interested in disaggregated benefits of policy choices, the distributive effects of monetary policy outcomes should captivate members of Congress. Members of Congress have imagined and proposed a monetary policy regime that would permit precise control over the distributive effects of monetary policy. The original Federal Reserve Act of 1913 anticipated qualitative management of the supply of money and credit as the primary function of the central bank. Under contemporary operating procedures, direct discussions of the distributive effects of monetary policy restraint or ease in FOMC meetings are reported to be quite rare (Woolley 1984). The deliberations over monetary policy institutions described in earlier chapters reveal, however, that concern about and attention to the distributive effects of monetary policy are routine. Board of Governors staff communications and reports routinely discuss anticipated and intended distributive effects of particular policy options, even if these effects were not specifically mentioned in FOMC minutes. Reserve requirement changes have been tied to increasing the share of available capital for lending for home mortgages and small business. Discount window borrowing practices have, at one time or another, been designed to redistribute credit and capital away from large business customers or consumers. Members of Congress recognize and act upon these distributive outcomes produced by monetary policy. Proposals to link reserve requirements to the composition of bank assets in the 1970s was tantamount to a demand from Congress for Fed allocation of credit across borrowers.

Observation of congressional behavior provides ample evidence for the salience of distributive demands in monetary policy debates. Congressional hearings on monetary policy have frequently been used as a forum for expressing the grievances of economic sectors dependent upon bank credit: small business, state and local government, and home buyers. Alt (1991) and Kettl (1986) report that members of Congress are most likely to introduce legislation threatening Fed autonomy or operations when rising nominal interest rates imposes costs on important classes of borrowers. Members of Congress routinely act upon narrow economic grievances in other policy domains. Birnbaum and Murray (1988) describe remarkable examples of legislative redistribution through the tax code in *Showdown at Gucci Gulch.* Rules ultimately included in the 1985 tax reform effort targeted very narrow benefits to very small groups. It would have been incredible if Congress created the Internal Revenue Service or reformed the tax code to simply generate the aggregate amount of money necessary to meet revenue requirements and failed to retained control over the distribution of the tax burden (Beck 1990(b)). To claim that members of Congress overlook or fail to appreciate the distributive consequences of monetary policy is equally incredible. Beck (1984) explains the claim behind descriptions of legislative behavior that predict congressional inattention.

> It also appears to assume that monetary policy can provide only collective, rather than particularistic, benefits; members of Congress, on the other hand, are interested in programs that can generate particularistic benefits. Monetary policy provides collective benefits at present because that is the way we have decided to conduct monetary policy. One could easily imagine a monetary policy based more on credit allocation (such as in France); at that point members of Congress could clearly benefit from becoming more active in the making of monetary policy. (Beck 1984, 815)

In the period of growing central bank autonomy after World War II, members of Congress simply responded to distributive consequences of monetary policy choices by creating new agencies, rather than engaging in some type of hierarchical control of monetary policy and direct credit allocation. Distributive goals are relevant to both members of Congress and to the White House. These distributive goals were never entirely detached from monetary policy choices nor were these distributive goals subordinated to macroeconomic objectives.

ALLOCATION OF CREDIT AND CAPITAL AFTER WORLD WAR II

Qualitative Allocation of Credit

Both members of Congress and presidents attempt to balance the conflicting goals of price stability and privileged access to capital. The set of monetary and credit policies that were preferred by elected officials after World War II implied a role for the central bank that is quite different from the type of central bank observed today. Institutional choices made within the Fed help to explain the divergence from the postwar model.

The Truman CEA defended selective regulation of credit terms as the best mechanism to lower interest rates and stimulate economic growth. This credit market strategy had a simple and compelling logic: preserve cheap bank credit for those industries and enterprises that provide essential services or meet essential needs and restrict the availability of credit for non-essential uses.[1] The problem with the strategy was the opposition to governmental regulation raised by "non-essential" borrowers. Members of the CEA failed to anticipate the political implications of a capital allocation program that coupled low interest rates with selective regulation. The low interest rate strategy articulated by Leon Keyserling and the Truman CEA provides a public good or collective benefit, low interest rates, to producers and bank borrowers. At the same time individual industries and businesses are burdened with costly regulatory restrictions. Selective regulations on consumer credit (administrative constraints on down payment terms and regulated interest rates on obligations) were intended to reduce the demand for credit among potential borrowers during periods of economic growth. The selective controls restrained purchasing during economic expansion, creating opposition among both potential lenders (home mortgage lenders, automobile manufacturers, consumer finance companies) and potential consumers (prospective buyers of automobiles, consumer durables, and homes). Political opposition to direct regulation was therefore both vocal and pervasive. The termination of most selective controls in 1952 reflected the political liabilities of selective regulation.

After the 1952 experience, the Eisenhower CEA began a study of selective controls as a cyclical restraint. Premature reports of new credit controls triggered immediate opposition from industries dependent upon credit finance. The set of policies that resulted from the termination of selective controls was a repudiation of the Truman credit market strategy. During the Eisenhower Administration, the central bank permitted interest rates to climb as high as necessary to restrain the growth of bank credit. Members of Congress and the White House advocated direct relief (administered independent of the monetary authority) to those most disadvantaged by high interest rates: prospective home owners, small businesses, and state and local government. Automobile manufacturers were a distinct and vocal loser in this arrangement. The General Motors' Acceptance Corporation, a private remedy to the increasing cost of bank borrowing, was the industry response.

Institutional changes after World War II (the repudiation of direct controls and use of the Bills Only Doctrine) limited the administrative capacity of the central bank to meet the distributive objectives of elected officials. Frustrated elected officials did not abdicate the task of indirect credit allocation to the central bank. Instead, elected officials created alternative institutions to address credit market objectives independent of the central bank. One of the most visible responses to the distributive effects of monetary policy choices has been legislative innovation in the form of credit programs for particular economic sectors: mortgage market support, small business finance, export finance, and student loans. These selective provisions of credit can protect particular sectors of the economy from the general monetary and credit policies of the central bank.

Real Effects of Government Intervention

Selective government intervention has taken the form of both loan guarantees and direct loans. Guarantees channel capital to specific economic sectors served by the commercial banking system. Direct loans provide credit to affected sectors independent of the commercial banking system. The magnitude of the economic effects of this type of government intervention in credit markets is the subject of considerable controversy among economists. Some observers suggest that capital market intervention produces real effects since capital markets are somewhat segmented. Proponents of the "segmented capital markets" approach argue that investors and borrowers operate in fairly narrow segments of the financial markets and that narrow market intervention can affect prices in each segmented market. Government can borrow from one segment of the capital market and lend in another segment and affect the relative price of credit. Rational expectations models of capital market behavior imply that this type of intervention is ineffective. Capital is mobile across markets, so investor and borrower adjustments across markets (and across securities with different maturities) will undo the efforts of government to allocate credit. Investors will adjust portfolios as government activity changes the relative prices of credit. Campbell and Shiller (1991) describe a variety of violations of expectations models that suggest substantial and continuing segmentation in the market for government securities. Kidwell and Koch (1983) and Simon (1991) find direct evidence of segmentation in other narrow money and capital markets. Bosworth, Carron & Rhyne (1987) conclude that contemporary financial markets are segmented in the short-term, but undifferentiated in the long-term. Portfolio adjustment is not immediate. If this conclusion is correct, then the real distributive effects of credit market intervention should be most visible in the early postwar period and diminish over time as the volume of funds moving across financial markets increases. The distributive goals of members of Congress are likely to be satisfied most immediately in the early experimentation with credit market programs. If Kidwell and Koch or Simon are correct, then federal credit programs have substantial real effects on the distribution of capital across borrowers.

OPPORTUNITIES TO DISTRIBUTE CAPITAL

Origins and Magnitude of Federal Credit Programs

Government intervention in capital markets was one component of government activity aimed at solving the economic problems of the Great Depression and preventing future prolonged economic downturns. The Depression revealed a number of failures in private capital markets that could be ameliorated by modest government risk underwriting, economies of scale introduced by government pools, or government regulation. Credit programs targeting agriculture, business, and the banking sector were introduced first to direct government relief to these sectors and later to improve the flow of funds to these sectors (Bosworth et al 1987). The volume of credit extended or guaranteed by government and the level of subsidy introduced by government varies substantially over these Depression-era programs.

Government intervention to meet the needs of two bank-dependent sectors of the economy—small business and home mortgage borrowers—demonstrates how actively elected officials reacted to changing capital market conditions in the postwar period. The remarkable growth of credit supplied to these two sectors of the economy is coincident with increasing central bank autonomy and increasing nominal interest rates. Each sector has benefited from government intervention in distinct ways. Credit for business has been relatively low in volume but heavily subsidized. Credit for the mortgage market has been high in volume but incorporated very little explicit subsidy. Both types of intervention were linked to the impact of monetary policy choices on borrowers. The failure of the Fed to remedy the selective effects of monetary restraint in these sectors of the economy motivated Congress to create new subsidy programs or expand existing programs.

Credit for the Mortgage Market

Support for the Mortgage Market

The federal government plays a significant and direct role in the allocation of capital to the residential mortgage market. Since the end of World War II, support for housing consumption has involved an extraordinary commitment of national resources. The residential mortgage market absorbs nearly 20 percent of all funds supplied to financial markets in the United States.[2] Low-interest direct Federal loans from the Federal Housing Administration and the Veterans Administration provide funds to needy borrowers. Prior to the reorganization of thrift institutions in 1990, loans to mortgage-lending institutions from the Federal Home Loan Bank Board provided special access to capital for thrift institutions. Federal Housing Administration and Veterans Administration insurance programs offer federal guarantees for primary mortgage market lenders. The federally-supported secondary market for existing loans guarantees a stable flow of funds into the mortgage market.

The federally-supported secondary market is the largest and most important type of federal intervention in the residential mortgage market. Three secondary market organizations supply most of the funds advanced in mortgage markets: the Federal National Mortgage Association (FNMA), the Government National Mortgage Association (GNMA), and the Federal Home Loan Mortgage Association (Freddie Mac). These agencies, collectively known as the federally-related mortgage pools, actively intervene in the secondary market for mortgages, matching savings from investors with returns from existing mortgages. The agencies buy pools of mortgages from lenders and sell shares in the stream of principal and interest payments to investors. The debt instruments purchased by investors are either explicitly or implicitly backed by the full faith and credit of the federal government, reducing the exposure of individual investors to loss. Each of the agencies purchase a specific type of mortgage. GNMA mortgage pools are composed of FHA-insured and VA-insured mortgages. FNMA mortgage pools include conventional mortgages. Freddie Mac purchases mortgages from member banks of the Federal Home Loan Bank System. The amount of home mortgage credit advanced under the auspices of the federal mortgage pools routinely exceeds seventy percent of total household borrowing in the mortgage market in any quarter. As a consequence of this brisk activity, the portfolio of mortgages held by the mortgage pools is valued at over $1.3 trillion.[3] The growth of the annual activity of the federal mortgage pools is displayed in Figure 9, below.

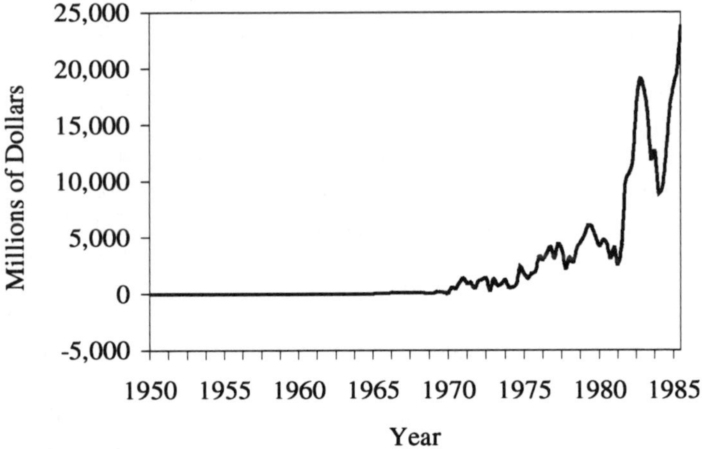

Figure 9
Quarterly purchases of residential mortgages by the federally-related mortgage pools (1950-1985).

Source: Flow of Funds Coded Tables.
Board of Governors of the Federal Reserve System.
See endnotes for additional information.

Objectives of Mortgage Market Intervention

Secondary mortgage market activity sponsored by the federal government has three basic goals: distribute capital across regions of the country, stabilize the supply of credit over the business cycle, and attract non-traditional investors to the mortgage market. A secondary market for mortgages increases mortgage market efficiency by removing barriers to the geographic flow of funds. By making the mortgage market the federal mortgage pools can smooth interest rates and the flow of funds across the nation. In practice, the outcomes may be less dramatic. Morrell and Saba (1983) argue that federal mortgage pool activity has little real effects on capital markets, but the administration of uniform mortgage contracts and underwriting practices makes secondary mortgage transactions less costly.

The secondary mortgage markets were originally developed to insulate the residential construction market from changes in the business cycle. Residential construction is pro-cyclical. Construction activity amplifies economic recessions and upturns. Residential construction is also an economic activity that is immediately influenced by changes in interest rates. Sensitivity of the residential construction sector to changes in interest rates creates a reliable transmission mechanism for monetary policy, but the impact of monetary policy is inconsistent with national housing goals (Buckley, Tuccillo & Villani, 1977). As Chairman of the CEA under Eisenhower, Arthur Burns advocated direct action by the Fed to exempt the housing sector from monetary policy restraint.[4] Staff at the National Bureau Of Economic Research reported on the consequences of these early subsidies in 1957:

> Housing is unquestionably the main economic sector in which the new political-economic environment has blunted the effectiveness of central bank policy. (An interesting historical question: Has housing in this report taken the place of the agricultural sector with its investment and politically powerful demands for cheap credit, while recent aids to agriculture have taken mainly forms other than cheap credit).[5]

By 1975 the amount of home mortgage credit advanced under the auspices of the federal government exceeded thirty percent of total mortgage financing—accounting for nearly one-third of all federal lending for any purpose.[6] As nominal interest rates rose above historic highs in the early 1970s, the mortgage market was offered some protection by pool purchases.

Managing Mortgage Market Intervention

Members of Congress have attempted on several occasions to integrate the Fed into the mortgage market directly. Congress granted the Fed statutory authority to purchase securities issued by the various federal agencies, anticipating purchases of notes issued by the FNMA. Congress granted the Board of Governors (and other bank regulators) authority to regulate interest rates on time and demand deposits. One goal was to protect thrift institutions, the principal source of primary mortgages before 1980. Finally, members of Congress proposed changes in reserve requirements that linked required reserves with bank assets. Implementation of asset-based reserve requirements would have encouraged banks to hold and purchase residential mortgages. The Fed initially supported interest rate regulation and engaged in modest purchases of agency issues consistent with mortgage market goals. Fed decision makers strongly resisted the use of reserve requirements to stimulate the flow of funds into mortgage markets. Absent direct Fed action to support the mortgage market, members of Congress permitted the volume of secondary mortgage market activity to increase over time.

Several powerful and narrow groups of economic actors are directly benefited by secondary mortgage market activity: mortgage lenders, real estate professionals, and home builders. If the federal mortgage pools actively purchase loans, then mortgage lenders can maintain a high volume of loans and transfer some of the underwriting risk to the federal mortgage pools. Abundant and cheap credit stimulates the construction and sale of homes. Real estate professionals are insulated from economic recession and the business of real estate benefits from high and stable home prices. Home builders are encouraged to take risks building new property. A mortgage lender does not need to ration credit locally when the federal mortgage pools provide a steady stream of subsidized capital. Each of these actors—real estate professionals, mortgage lenders, and home builders—benefits from persistent and growing supply of capital to finance the purchase and construction of homes.

Management of the federally-related mortgage pools creates a dilemma for federal policy makers. Kaufman (1988) explains that policy makers have two choices: accept risk or accept market outcomes. Policy makers may instruct mortgage pool managers to accept financial risk. Acceptance of risk subsidizes mortgage credit and redistributes savings from unsubsidized sectors of the capital market to the mortgage market. Policy makers could instead choose to instruct federal mortgage pool managers to compete directly, without subsidy, with private suppliers of funds and minimize redistribution of capital towards the mortgage market. In order to pursue national housing goals, the federal mortgage pools must accept some risk and, at least implicitly, offer subsidies to risky buyers. Given the volume of mortgage purchases by the pools, even a small implicit subsidy has substantial real effects.

Credit for Small Business Enterprise

Origins of Protection for Small Business

The Truman White House solicited informal cooperation from Fed Chairman Thomas McCabe to provide special credit assistance to small business in 1950.[7] Informal and voluntary regional credit restraint programs administered by the Fed were expected to direct credit disproportionately to small business enterprise. Later, Dwight Eisenhower established a Cabinet Committee on Small Business to coordinate aid to small business across the various federal agencies. Dissatisfied with the accomplishments of the voluntary programs and other informal measures, members of Congress created the Small Business Administration (SBA). The SBA was originally proposed as a temporary program to remedy a shortage of bank credit that threatened small business enterprise. Under the Small Business Act of 1958, the SBA was made permanent and endowed with authority to issue direct loans to small business and guarantee private loans to small business.[8]

The SBA loan guarantee program is the largest source of federal subsidy to small business enterprise. Obligations of the Small Business Administration expanded substantially in real terms after the agency was given permanent authority to guarantee loans. During periods of extraordinary monetary restraint (and high nominal interest rates) SBA subsidy activity has directed subsidized capital to a broad range of business constituents. The SBA made a particular effort to encourage long-term lending to small business borrowers in the 1970s.[9] The total dollar amount of loans guaranteed annually under 7(a) authority grew from under $50 million in 1958 to over $3 billion by 1980.[10] Estimates prepared by the General Accounting Office indicate that SBA participation extended to over 30 percent of bank and industrial loans to small business borrowers by 1980 (Bosworth et al 1987).

Objectives of Small Business Credit Subsidy

The primary problem that motivated Congress to create the SBA guarantee program was poor access to capital for small business. Small businesses generally have access only to traditional forms of credit offered by banks. The dependence of small business borrowers on bank credit creates capital market advantages for large business borrowers that have access to equity financing or other sources of capital. Lenders also charge interest rate premiums (or ration capital) to potential small business borrowers since small business ventures are risky. Loan guarantees remedy the disparity between large business and small business. Rhyne (1988) notes that loans guaranteed by SBA have longer maturities than non-SBA loans to similar businesses. The SBA can effectively address the credit gap between large business borrowers and small business competitors. This subsidy corrects some of the perverse selective effects of monetary restraint that frustrated the White House, particularly CEA Chairman Arthur Burns, in the 1950s.

Credit for small business borrowers is particularly sensitive to monetary restraint and turns in the business cycle. Since small borrowers are rarely offered the same lending terms as large firms, monetary restraint typically disrupts the flow of capital to small business before affecting large business customers. SBA loan guarantees can create incentives for financial institutions to make loans that would otherwise appear unattractive. The prospective costs of default on a risky loan are absorbed by the federal government.

Economic research on the SBA has focused on the ability of SBA to use loan guarantees to counteract the influence of the business cycle on small business enterprise. The SBA clearly faces a major problem meeting this objective: poor economic conditions deter prospective small business owners from seeking bank financing. Loan demand may dominate policy objectives in determining loan guarantee levels. This problem is identified by Bosworth et al (1987) as an obstacle to SBA performance of counter-cyclical goals. The original objectives of credit subsidies to small business, to stabilize credit over the business cycle and provide credit to the neediest borrowers, require that the supply of loans be largest when economic and credit market conditions are poor. Since loan demand is highest when the economy is growing, the supply of loan guarantees may respond in the opposite direction desired by policy makers.

Costs of SBA Subsidy Activity

The real effects of the loan guarantee program on small business enterprise are unclear. The SBA 7(a) program is nevertheless quite popular and not subjected to considerable fiscal restraint. Ippolito (1984) examined SBA expenditures in a broader analysis of the many federal credit programs that escape budgetary scrutiny due to the accounting treatment of loans. The vast majority of SBA subsidy takes the form of loan guarantees, a particularly difficult practice to subject to strict budgetary control. Loan guarantees may be costless if the pool of loans given guarantees is small and low risk. Loan guarantees may be costly if the pool of loans is large and risky. In any case, loan guarantees carry small short-term costs and uncertain long-term costs. This feature makes guarantees attractive for any political actor that discounts the future. Other social actors favor small business subsidies as well. It should be no surprise that commercial bank lenders strongly encourage the growth and maintenance of the guarantee programs (Rhyne 1988). Government loan guarantees generate new business and increase loan volume for bank. The risks of default are absorbed by the federal government. Elected officials and lenders (and agency managers) benefit if guarantee programs grow and persist.

PROLIFERATION OF FEDERAL CREDIT SUBSIDY

The widespread (and ostensibly unselective) application of monetary restraint encourages borrowers from credit-dependent sectors to petition for relief from market competition for bank credit. Members of Congress have been willing to establish programs that at least provide some relief from high interest rates. The reluctance of decision makers within the Fed to specifically shelter particular classes of borrowers compelled Congress to rely on credit programs that have proved difficult to control and that generate economic results that may be undesirable. The task of allocating credit is fraught with both political problems and economic obstacles. The affected sectors often enjoy considerable interest representation in Washington D.C. and, in the case of the home-building industry, a substantial grassroots constituency. Innovations in financial markets and institutions make it increasingly difficult for credit allocation to affect credit flows without substantial subsidies to borrowers.

It is not surprising that decision makers in the central bank updated instruments to avoid a direct role in credit allocation. As Chairman of the Board of Governors of the Federal Reserve System, Arthur Burns made the case against central bank credit allocation before the House Subcommittee on Domestic Monetary Policy in 1976:

> Decisions as to social priorities in the use of credit are inherently political in character. If such decisions are to be made at all, they should be made by Congress—not by an administrative and non-political body such as the Federal Reserve. After all, tilting credit in favor of some borrowers implies denying credit to someone else. Our economy has developed by relying on the market to make such decisions.[11]

This reluctance to engage in the allocation of credit is consistent with updates to operating procedure made after World War II. But the rhetoric of the virtues of the private market and impersonal allocation of capital through the market does not fully explain the position of Arthur Burns or other Fed actors. It is not reliance on private market mechanisms that repels the Fed from direct allocation, but the threats to autonomy that would accompany allocation. Scrutiny of Fed choices by Congress would undermine the autonomy of the central bank.

The reluctance of decision makers in the Fed to accept a role in credit allocation has not discouraged members of Congress from intervening in capital markets. Over time, the magnitude of federal intervention in capital markets has become staggeringly large. Federal credit programs distribute narrow benefits to particular groups and diffuse costs (in the form of marginally higher interest rates) across a number of borrowers. Members of Congress face no real constraints from the central bank in the creation and operation of these discrete credit market programs. The proliferation of federal credit programs is not, however, without costs.

The Problem of Control

A 1969 Committee to Reappraise Federal Credit Programs evaluated the operation of rapidly growing federal direct lending and guarantee programs. The Committee report advocated the judicious use of loan guarantees, rather than federal direct lending to subsidize particular economic functions.[12] Loan guarantees minimize the government role in loan transactions: lending professionals process loans, screen applicants and oversee collection of debts. The trade-off is the problem of moral hazard. Hunter (1984) identifies a severe moral hazard problem in the loan guarantee program of the Small Business Administration. The federal government does not control the costs related to loan guarantees. Lenders select borrowers from the pool of potential applicants. Borrower behavior determines if the loan performs or fails. The future costs of present subsidies are jointly determined by the decisions of the lender and the borrower, not by the guarantor. The presence of this type of moral hazard, coupled with poor budgetary accounting of the real costs of guarantees, has resulted in a large subsidy for small businesses seeking capital (Bosworth et al 1987). Recent efforts to reduce administrative costs of loans programs have identified the proliferation of loan guarantees as an expensive solution to credit shortages.

Implications of Program Expansion

The growth of federal credit programs has attracted the scrutiny of economists for a number of reasons. Early growth of credit programs was thought to blunt the transmission of monetary policy. Aaron (1972) claimed that purchases of mortgages by the federally-related mortgage pools delayed the impact of restrictive monetary policy in 1966. If the federal mortgage pools can mitigate the impact of Fed policy choices on mortgage interest rates, then the Fed would lose an important channel for the implementation of monetary restraint. Historic peaks of nominal interest rates on home mortgages in the 1980s revealed that Fed policy choices could ultimately overwhelm even massive intervention by the mortgage pools.

As federal credit programs continue to expand, the critical focus has turned from macroeconomic implications of credit subsidies to the actuarial soundness of government intervention. Peterson (1993) and others have claimed that the growth of middle-class entitlements, persistent budget deficits, and poor financial management of federal assets threatens fiscal solvency in the future. Most of these claims are ignored simply because the deficit and entitlement growth have persisted for so long without obvious ill effects on economic performance and, quite recently, the size of the unified budget deficit has declined. The consequences of the federal government absorbing hidden financial risks have, on the other hand, been quite overt. The mismanagement of savings and loans in the early 1980s cost the taxpayers an extraordinary sum. Lessons from the failure of some Depression-era credit subsidies also points to problems with risk underwriting by government. The failure of the Federal Farm Land Bank in 1933 has been linked to federal acceptance of excessive risk in capital markets (O'Hara 1983). The combined portfolios of the federally-related mortgage pools already greatly exceed one trillion dollars. Economic fluctuations that produce unusually high rates of default on home mortgages could expose the federal government to tremendous liabilities on these debt instruments. As the federal role continues to expand, this risk is increased.

Unintended Consequences of Subsidy Activity

One probable consequence of a continuous supply of cheap and abundant credit to subsidize home mortgages is increases in the price of homes. This unintended consequence of intervention has frustrated federal credit subsidy programs in the past. O'Hara (1983) concludes that Federal Farm Land Bank, intended to abet farm finance for tenant farmers in the 1900s, increased the price of land and created a windfall for current landowners. Farm tenancy rates fell as the market for farm loans was dominated by the federal lending agencies. The price of land rose as abundant cheap credit drove competition for existing land. The redistributive impact of intervention—favoring current landowners and hurting prospective land buyers—was not an intentional consequence of the policy choice. Treasury staff reviewing the effects of housing credit programs in 1974 argued that federal credit programs contributed to "the explosion of land, labor, and material costs."[13] Student loans subsidies have been similarly implicated in the extraordinary increase in the costs of college education after 1970.

State Intervention in Capital Markets

Central bank decision makers have identified the significant role of government in credit allocation as a severe source of distortion in capital markets.[14] Federal guarantee and insurance programs divert capital from "market-worthy" channels to state-sponsored borrowers. Concerns about interference with market allocation motivated Treasury staff to oppose further action to increase the number of federal credit programs to alleviate housing credit shortages in 1974. In fact, under the Ford Administration the Treasury advocated dismantling existing programs to return more market restraint to credit markets.[15] These types of reservations have been used by the Fed to oppose the inclusion of credit allocation functions in the Federal Reserve Act, but not to challenge the credit allocation through existing agencies. At the same time that Treasury staff questioned the utility of federal credit programs in 1974, Arthur Burns applauded existing programs and urged members of Congress to develop more federal credit programs to solve the disruptions created by restrictive monetary policy.[16] Burns position on credit allocation and the economic utility of redistribution is different, of course, depending on what agencies, the Fed or government-sponsored enterprises, directly intervene in capital markets. Fed allocation is anathema; other government-sponsored intervention is desirable. A direct role in credit allocation threatens central bank autonomy.

CONCLUSION AND SUMMARY

In the original Federal Reserve Act of 1913 the central bank was expected to routinely allocate credit across borrowers. Speculative borrowing was to be discouraged; lending that contributed to production and manufacturing was to be encouraged. After World War II, the Board of Governors of the Federal Reserve System was similarly expected to administer direct controls that restricted credit for particular economic functions. Credit for desirable and productive activities was expected to be available at a low rate of interest. Poor experience with the qualitative allocation of credit and the administration of direct selective controls led central bank decision makers to update monetary policy institutions. Open market operating practices adopted under Eisenhower foreclosed direct allocation of capital across borrowers. Indirect reserve instruments and discount window lending guidelines permitted covert distribution of credit, but overt allocation was not expected to occur under the new operating practices. As a consequence of the procedural choices of the central bank and rising costs of borrowing, members of Congress created new programs to counteract efforts to restrain the economy with monetary policy. These new programs permitted members of Congress (and occupants of the White House) to meet particular distributive goals without threatening the independent status of the central bank. As the central bank continued to update operating procedures to enhance autonomy, the scope and size of federal credit programs expanded. With the exception of the purchase of FNMA issues by the Fed in the 1970s, the Fed avoided direct intervention in the capital markets targeted for protection by Congress. The Fed gained substantial autonomy to achieve the goal of price stability; members of Congress realized the benefits of federal credit programs. The drawbacks of the credit programs—redistributive costs and real costs—are poorly understood and rarely a liability for an individual member of Congress. Only the president, lacking the formal tools to bring about preferred macroeconomic outcomes from the central bank and lacing direct control over capital market outcomes, is seriously disadvantaged by increasing central bank autonomy in the conduct of monetary policy.

NOTES

1. These objectives also describe the original Federal Reserve Act. This "qualitative" distribution of credit is described in Chapter 5.

2. Credit market data summarized in this discussion are obtained from the *Flow of Funds* tables produced by the Board of Governors of the Federal Reserve System. See related notes in Chapter 4 for more information on the flow of funds.

3. *Budget of the United States Government.* Fiscal Year 1995. Analytical Perspectives. Washington D.C.: United States Government.

4. AFB Talk. 16 November 1956. Folder*: Talk on Credit Restraint, Given at Cabinet Meeting.* Papers of Arthur F. Burns. Box #76. Dwight D. Eisenhower Library

5. Notes for A.F. Burns on Housing Credit, 1953-57. Prepared by Leo Grebler at the National Bureau of Economic Research in 1957. Folder: *Housing Credit: 1956.* Box #109. Papers of Arthur Burns. Eisenhower Library.

6. Memo. 10 January 1975. Roy Ash to the President. Folder: *FA 5. Housing.* Box #13. White House Central Files. Gerald R. Ford Library.

7. Letter. 7 March 1950. Thomas McCabe to Stephen Springarn. Folder: *Finance and Industry. Small Business Programs.* Box #15. Papers of Stephen Springarn. Harry S Truman Library.

8. Second Report by the Cabinet Committee on Small Business. 31 December 1958. Folder: *OF 122-O-1 Cabinet Committee on Small Business (2).* White House Central Files. Official Files. Dwight D. Eisenhower Library.

9. Memo. Thomas Kleppe, Administrator of the SBA, to Donald Rumsfeld, Assistant to the President. 6 December 1974. Folder: *FI 5-6. Small Business.* Box #22. White House Central Files. Gerald R. Ford Library.

10. *Catalog of Federal Domestic Assistance.* 59.012 Small Business Loans. Washington, D.C.: United States Government.

11. Statement of Arthur Burns before the House Subcommittee on Domestic Monetary Policy. 6 February 1975. Folder: *FG 39-9. Joint Economic Committee.* Box #135. White House Central Files. Gerald R. Ford Library.

12. Report of the Committee to Reappraise Federal Credit Programs. 25 April 1969. Folder: *Federal Credit Programs.* White House Series. Box # A10. Papers of Arthur Burns. Gerald R. Ford Library.

13. Treasury Economic Policy Issue Paper. 21 September 1974. Folder: *Economic Policy Input—Treasury.* Counsellors to the President. Paul McCracken. Box #4. Gerald R. Ford Library.

14. Memo. Division of Research and Statistics to Chairman Burns. 11 November 1976. Folder: *Reuss, Henry. October—December, 1976.* Congressional Correspondence. Box #O16. Papers of Arthur Burns. Gerald R. Ford Library.

15. Treasury Economic Policy Issue Paper. 21 September 1974. Folder: *Economic Policy Input—Treasury.* Counsellors to the President. Paul McCracken. Box #4. Gerald R. Ford Library.

16. Letter. Arthur Burns to Henry Reuss. 29 July 1974. Folder: *Reuss, Henry. January 1972—January 1975.* Congressional Correspondence. Box # 016. Papers of Arthur Burns. Gerald R. Ford Library.

CHAPTER 8

Representative Control of Monetary Policy

Monetary policy institutions are not simply technical rules designed to increase the precision of monetary control in complex financial markets. Institutions that structure choice and action within agencies have strategic and political utility for agency decision makers. These institutions can condition the relationship between an agency and social actors with a stake in agency outcomes. One implication of this dual role for agency procedures is apparent from Fed experience. Strategic considerations may challenge precision or efficiency considerations as policy institutions are updated.

The central bank in the United States enjoys a remarkable level of autonomy. This autonomy has increased over time and is quite surprising given the strict administrative subordination of the monetary authority to the Treasury after World War II. The benefits and costs of central bank autonomy are the subject of an ongoing debate in the economic literature. Most recent work finds considerable merit in the maintenance and protection of central bank autonomy (Alesina and Gatti 1995, McCallum 1995, Fisher 1995). The direct role that central bank decision makers play in the maintenance of autonomy has been given scant attention in this debate. Most scholarship identifies central bank autonomy as a function of formal legal rules or terms of appointment, rather than a function of the procedural choices of central bankers (Grilli, Masciandaro & Tabellini 1991, Cukierman, Webb & Neyapti 1994, Schaling 1995). The postwar experience of the United States suggests that this formal legalistic approach is misleading and insufficient. The political strategy of the U.S. central bank, implemented in fairly static formal legal environment, determines central bank autonomy. In the United States, central bank autonomy increases without formal institutional change.

The strategy adopted by the Fed to maintain autonomy has two components. First, decision makers avoid rules that affect economic sectors singled out for protection by Congress. Second, if sector-specific intervention is a necessity, central bankers use indirect instruments to transmit restraint or stimulus through money and capital markets. The central bank restrains lending only covertly through bank financial institutions. This minimizes overt conflict over central bank choices that influence the allocation of money and credit across financial markets. In short, monetary policy institutions are designed and updated to minimize political conflict over the distribution of monetary restraint across capital and money markets. Procedural choices related to each set of domestic monetary policy instruments confirms that central bankers update instruments in ways that minimize incentives for members of Congress to redistribute capital with monetary policy.

The series of institutional changes undertaken to implement and refine this strategy has patent effects on congressional supervision of monetary policy. Restrictive rules encourage members of Congress to develop alternatives to central bank monetary policy institutions. Weak direct redistribution by the central bank creates incentives for legislators to directly assist particular sectors by subsidizing loans and credit. Changes in monetary policy institutions help to explain a number of features of contemporary monetary politics: the limits of hierarchical control, the failure of efforts to systematically allocate credit across economic functions, and limits to political control of macroeconomic outcomes. Changes in Fed practice also underscore the problem of reform and the dilemma posed by political control of monetary policy. Any reform effort that places the Fed under the political control of elected officials promises to increase executive control over monetary policy choices. Political control, in practice, has taken the form of executive influence over regulatory actions (in the case of direct controls) and executive coordination of market intervention. Members of Congress and decision makers in the Fed share the goal of avoiding this type of executive control over monetary policy.

INSTITUTIONS AND INCREMENTAL CHANGE

The continuous development of central bank operating practices is a consequence of both technical innovation and interactions with elected officials. Changes in the structure and integration of financial markets compels Fed policy makers to update operating procedures. Efforts to bring monetary and capital markets under political control compel Fed policy makers to update operating procedures. Both imperatives foreclose the use of one set of instruments or one approach to monetary policy for long periods of time. Between 1948 and 1980 there were frequent changes in the definition of required reserves, discount window borrowing conventions, and, less frequently, changes in rules governing open market activity. This process of change and revision is not a process that could be described as either approaching or representing some type of equilibrium. Agency practices are highly variable.

Baumgartner and Jones (1990) describe institutional change in American politics as an example of punctuated equilibrium, a model of evolutionary change developed by paleobiologists (Eldredge and Gould 1972). Baumgartner and Jones demonstrate how jurisdictional monopolies in Congress, media coverage of issues, and interest group activity are fairly stable for long periods of time. Important changes in policy choice can occur if either group representation, media coverage, or congressional jurisdictions are altered. Typically, changes in one area lead to changes in another and the pace of change is rapid. Institutional stasis is punctuated by short bursts of change. Skowronek (1982) also describes institutional change in American politics as a series of changes that, in a short period of time at the beginning of the century, radically transformed domestic politics. This description of rapid change does not fit the central bank or the politics of monetary policy. Change in agency practice and procedure is continuous and incremental. Signal reform and rehabilitation of formal rules never occurs, despite dramatic changes in the financial and political environment of policy choices over time. Punctuated equilibrium fails to describe change at the central bank simply because many important choices about institutions and outcomes are made within the agency and not debated or approved by Congress. Fairly broad procedural discretion leads to substantive autonomy.

One implication of slowly changing agency practice is opportunity for experimentation and innovation. Some institutional change at the Fed is undone after a brief period. Selective controls on mortgage credit, for instance, were expected to greatly facilitate implementation of monetary policy during the Korean mobilization. After the benefits of the controls were compared to the political problems of implementation and oversight, the selective regulations were terminated. The rules were updated fairly quickly. This experience does not mean that institutional changes at the agency level are without costs. Institutional change at the Fed is typically justified as a logical consequence of changes in either the structure of financial markets (a technical necessity) or changes in economic theory (a rational update). Policy makers at the Fed invest considerable effort to ensure that outcomes and choices are perceived as objective responses to changing economic and financial market conditions. Wholesale changes in operating procedures would challenge the credibility of the technical and economic claims that accompany institutional changes.

The process of institutional change characteristic of punctuated equilibrium models, rapid and producing consequential change in outcomes, limits opportunities for strategic actors to control the direction of change. The foresight of social actors interested in updating institutions is severely limited by poor information about the behavior of others under new rules and the ultimate consequences of change. Punctuated equilibrium models of institutional change imply that strategic social actors occasionally participate in a process of change that produces unforeseen outcomes. Social actors will accept loss of control over outcomes in exchange for a challenge to the status quo. From this perspective, institutional change at the Fed is extremely conservative. Fed decision makers only incrementally update institutions. For technical and strategic reasons, central bank decision makers never radically update monetary policy institutions.

Despite the conservative and incremental nature of change at the Fed, the sequence of choices made within the Fed transformed the central bank in ways that social actors will a stake in central bank outcomes would fail to anticipate. Neither the architects of the original Federal Reserve Act nor the White House staff under President Truman would advocate updates to monetary policy institutions that divorced questions of credit allocation from decisions over the supply of money to financial markets. Central bank decision makers prefer that the two policy choices be strictly separated: the preferred outcome for central bankers comes about as the product of gradual institutional change.

LIMITS OF HIERARCHICAL CONTROL

Decision makers at the Fed are able to exert some control over the set of incentives and restraints that influence the actions of elected officials. This capacity to update rules in a way that maximizes autonomy offers a formidable challenge to proponents of hierarchical control of bureaucracy as either a normative or practical answer to the challenge of delegation. A number of recent contributions to the study of policy and oversight have relied on principal-agent models to describe the relationship between elected officials and public sector managers (Wood and Waterman 1994). This class of models has also become quite popular as a way to describe the challenges, constraints, and choices facing and voters engaged in supervision of elected officials. As descriptive tools, principal-agent models make sense of the universe of exchange relationships that are the basis of politics (Spiller 1990). The key insight of the principal-agent literature applied to the problem of agency control is that elected officials often gain both electoral and substantive policy benefits from the delegation of authority to a bureaucratic agent.

Most of the formal principal-agent literature excludes by assumption the strategic alternatives of bureaucrats facing oversight and supervision in this context. Canonical agency theory presumes the existence of a contract—constructed and written by the principal—in order to ensure that the preferences of the agent are identical to the preferences of the principal. For a number of reasons, public agency fails to mirror the canonical principal-agent problem. Agencies are rarely dismantled or absorbed by competitors. Poor agency performance rarely results in the termination of career staff. Statutory direction never approaches the specificity of a contract. Finally, if a public agent is self-financing then most threats by a political principal are not credible. The costs of constructing statutory institutions to replace existing agencies are prohibitive except in truly extraordinary cases. The costs of constructing very specific statutory rules is also high, leaving the vast majority of rule-making at the discretion of bureaucratic agents. Strategic public agents exploit this discretion in unanticipated ways.

Recent reviews by Worsham, Eisner & Ringquist (1997) and Spence (1997) identify the assumptions and modeling approaches that have been adopted by proponents of the canonical principal-agent framework in political science. The real politics of agency control—collective action problems in Congress, conflict between executive and Congress, and strategic behavior of agents motivated by goals and objectives beyond simple budget maximization—are not critical components of the formal and empirical work that informs principal-agent approaches. As a consequences, principal-agent models of bureau politics do not capture the complexity of the strategic action that explains many of the institutional changes within agencies. The implications of these institutional choices are not trivial in this context. Procedural choices by the bureaucrat may encourage or constrain political principals with a variety of electoral and ideological objectives. Elected officials are then motivated to use existing agencies for new functions or to create new agencies to challenge the jurisdiction of existing agencies. Existing work provides little insight into this process.

The case of the Fed indicates that the strategic action of agency decision makers is a serious challenge to models of strict hierarchical control. Autonomy is clearly an important motivation for Fed actors. The two cases of strategic action described in Chapter 2 demonstrated how decision makers in the Fed pursued autonomy at the expense of other goals. Key actors in the Fed refused regulatory authority over thrifts in the 1970s. Reserve Bank presidents and the Board of Governors rejected the expansion of bank supervisory or regulatory authority, fearing that broader responsibility would jeopardize autonomy. Fed decision makers also resisted innovation in congressional oversight. Members of the Board of Governors objected to a variety of congressional oversight mechanisms (particularly expenditure ceilings and audits) as part of an ongoing struggle to divorce monetary policy outcomes from disputes over distribution of capital and credit. In neither case did central bank bureaucrats behave as either budget-maximizers or subordinate agents of Congress. Central bankers seek autonomy and discretion in ways that neither budget maximization nor political control models can predict or explain.

The case of the Fed also indicates that conflict between the executive and Congress, as well as disagreements in Congress, can be exploited by central bankers. Ferejohn and Shipan (1991) demonstrated how judicial review, amendments, and the executive veto undermine the oversight and control capabilities of committees in Congress. Fed decision makers directly exploit conflict between the White House and the Congress over control of monetary policy. In 1978, members of Congress and the White House staff simultaneously attempted to obtain more formal control over monetary policy outcomes. Congress considered updating the Federal Reserve Act under the Federal Reserve Reform Act of 1977. The White House endorsed rules requiring Fed-White House coordination of monetary policy under the Full Employment and Balanced Growth Act of 1978 (Humphrey-Hawkins). As both measures were debated, Board of Governors staff noted an advantage for the Fed.

> The play between these competing forces has given us very useful maneuvering flexibility that has assisted in the accomplishment of our legislative ends.[1]

Conflict between members of Congress and the executive over ultimate macroeconomic outcomes affects decisions about control and intervention in monetary policy. Conflict between members of Congress and the executive over capital market outcomes affects the creation and expansion of federal credit programs. If the monetary policy preferences of members of Congress and the White House diverge, then hierarchical control of the Fed or influence over operating procedures is difficult to achieve, either formally or informally. It is unlikely to be the case that precise and effective hierarchical controls can be engineered by Congress to bring about both desired macroeconomic and distributive outcomes using the central bank. Ferejohn (1986) showed how legislators could exploit the diverse preferences of a heterogeneous electorate to escape political control: agency decision makers can exploit diverse preferences of potential monitors in similar ways. Multiple committees in Congress respond to Fed action. Partisan disagreements weaken the capacity of members of Congress to exercise strict control over macroeconomic outcomes or systematically allocate credit. Recent experience indicates that members of Congress do realize the benefits of delegation in the form of price stability and obstacles to White House macroeconomic manipulation, but the delegation of monetary policy does not produce clear and immediate distributive gains.

CONTROL OVER MACROECONOMIC OUTCOMES: POLITICAL AND PARTISAN BUSINESS CYCLES

Institutional changes at the Fed have had a specific consequence that is often overlooked in the literature on monetary politics. The rules used to implement monetary policy encourage members of Congress to circumvent monetary restraint by creating agencies to protect specific sectors of the economy from the costs of monetary restraint. I draw two implications from this congressional activity. First, expectations of uniform political business cycles can never be realized. An increasing variety of agencies and quasi-governmental financial intermediaries must act in concert with the central bank to produce the types of capital and money market outcomes consistent with cyclical variation in macroeconomic outcomes. Second, federal credit programs will proliferate. As long as the central bank is somewhat autonomous, members of Congress will have strong incentives to create or sponsor agencies that provide credit and capital to particular sectors of the economy.

Elected officials cannot commit the Fed to a particular set of monetary policy choices. Absent this type of control mechanism, it is highly unlikely that elected officials can bring about preferred macroeconomic outcomes consistent with political business cycle or partisan business cycle theories. The paucity of controls is not a consequence of either formal rules that diminish the capacity of elected officials or problems of information or coordination. The rules adopted by central bank decision bankers foreclose precise and direct control by elected officials. These institutions reduce the chance of explicit legislative direction of central bank intervention in capital and money markets. Constraints on macroeconomic adjustment are byproducts of the institutions created to manage conflict over the distribution of capital.

One implication of the relatively weak influence of elected officials on monetary policy choices is exceptional reliance on fiscal policy to produce short-term changes in macroeconomic outcomes. Mebane (1994) reports variation in the payroll tax component of transfer programs consistent with increasing personal income near elections. Payroll taxes are reduced near elections. If executive manipulation of macroeconomic outcomes is accomplished using this type of mechanism, then precise control is immensely complicated by congressional budget procedures and tax laws. Central bank intransigence, a function of distributive conflict, coupled with distributive conflict over budget choices severely limits executive control of macroeconomic outcomes.

Havrilesky (1987) attributes change in monetary policy to fiscal policy choices that are jointly determined by members of Congress and the White House. He claims that the Fed observes and responds to the distributive fiscal policy bargains struck by members of Congress and the president. The Fed implements monetary policy conditional on fiscal policy choices. If this is the case, then members of Congress have very weak incentives to improve formal controls over monetary policy. Formal control mechanisms would simply invite executive challenges for control of monetary policy choices and possibly jeopardize the distributive arrangements engineered by Congress. Members of Congress have unilateral control over federal credit programs and a substantial influence (shared with the White House) over the distribution of resources in the budget. Existing arrangements ensure that members of Congress can indirectly obtain desired distributive outcomes, while presidents face severe constraints on macroeconomic policy choices.

POLITICAL ALLOCATION OF CAPITAL

Specific segments of capital markets are uniquely dependent on particular forms of credit. Bank-dependent sectors are particularly vulnerable to monetary restraint. As a consequence, central bank operating procedures can affect the relative price of credit for particular economic sectors. Central bankers apparently share many of the preferences of other social actors that have a stake in these capital market outcomes. Postwar monetary policy choices suggest that central bank decision makers prefer price stability to prolonged inflation, economic growth to recession, an orderly flow of funds to meet important social objectives such as adequate housing, and stable markets for government securities. Central bank decision makers may at times be compelled to take action or prefer to take action that favors one group over another, that redistributes scarce capital market resources from one group of borrowers to another, or that redistributes income from borrowers to lenders. In making these choices, the central bank in the United States has not been compelled to adopt rules that always benefit one group over another. There are no reserve requirements on assets that could lead to lower interest rates for home buyers. There are no open market rules that compel the central bank to purchase agency issues for the central bank portfolio. The rules do not systematically favor one particular group, but instead reserve discretion for central bank decision makers.

Statutory direction to redistribute credit from one segment of capital markets to another would imply that Congress engages in some kind of systematic evaluation of the merits of the demand for capital from specific economic actors. Instead, efforts to reconcile competing demands for credit across federal programs or to centralize management of credit subsidies in an agency like the Office of Management and Budget are never observed. Members of Congress protect and expand discrete, narrow credit subsidies. They do not choose to centralize credit allocation in any one agency, the Fed or a new agency that could be effectively subjected to executive control. The occasional use of Fed instruments, such as open market transactions, to pursue selective or narrow objectives is a substitute for the creation of permanent (statutory) rules to protect particular economic sectors. Members of Congress do not update Fed statutes to refine the formal mechanisms of control in order to affect specific distributive goals. The same formal changes could abet White House control over monetary policy. Members of Congress do not update the institutions of monetary policy in ways that explicitly and permanently protect narrow classes of borrowers, such as homeowners.

Critics of an autonomous central bank argue that independence from representative oversight simply reinforces the preferences of wealth-holders and commercial bankers (Greider 1987). Epstein and Schor (1989) describe representative control of monetary policy as an alternative to control by owners of capital. If representative control weakens, the influence of owners of capital increases. Labor and consumer interests are notable losers if representative control diminishes. The evidence presented does not support this type of dichotomy. Central bank decision makers do not adopt instruments that systematically favor one group over another. Instruments vary over time in ways that at time benefit borrowers (especially home buyers), at times favor large commercial banks, and at times favors smaller, rural banks. The rules never systematically and permanently redistribute capital or resources. Explicit redistributive choices and the political allocation of capital by the central bank would jeopardize and undermine central bank autonomy. The institutional changes that minimize incentives for representative control also reduce the ability of narrow organized social interests outside of government to influence monetary policy choices.

CHANGING THE TERMS OF POLITICAL CONTROL

Skowronek (1982) describes expansion of federal administrative capacity in the first two decades of the twentieth century as a response to the urgent demands of industrial and political development. He argues that these changes were a fundamental re-negotiation of the institutions of government and that these institutional changes function as boundaries or constraints on contemporary social actors. The experience of the central bank indicates that the administrative institutions of the federal government can accommodate a wide variety of outcomes and behavior: there is some substantial change under the re-negotiated institutions. The institutional arrangement that was constructed in the first two decades of the twentieth century accommodates a passive central bank or an autonomous central bank, a small and inconsequential White House staff or a large and institutionalized White House, a weak and ineffectual committee system in Congress or an attentive and well-informed Congress. The broader institutional arrangement identified by Skowronek, a new and powerful bureaucracy that challenges executive control and congressional monitoring capacities, creates incentives for the executive branch to increase control, for Congress to intervene, and, most important for my purposes, for agency managers to seek autonomy. Skowronek anticipates that fundamental reform may be difficult or impossible for elected officials interested in containing bureaucracies. Efforts to control bureaucracy are likely to result in "incremental reform, partial institutional breakthroughs, and untimely stalemates." (Skowronek 1982, 292) The gradual process of institutional change in the Fed reveals how the relationship between elected officials and the agencies may change dramatically over time, despite the presence of fairly stable formal rules governing agency structure and objectives.

North(1990) observed that institutional changes can, over time, produce radical divergence in economic performance across nations. The institutional changes that we observe in the central bank have effects on the distribution of wealth and income, as well as rate of economic growth and stability of financial markets. If it was possible to assess the preferences of social actors that had a stake in monetary policy outcomes after World War II and in the 1950s, it is difficult to imagine that they would prescribe the types of changes made at the central bank. The extension of open market operations to long-term securities failed to address the balance of payments problem. Complex reserve requirement creates an acute attrition problem for the System. Severe inflation in the 1970s revealed how poorly central bank decision makers understood the origins and control of price stability. Despite these overt problems, occasional challenges to Fed autonomy from loosely organized members of Congress, and open debate about the role of the central bank in credit allocation there have been no serious attempts to update the formal institutions of the central bank in a way that would change the contemporary terms of political control.

Congressional Intervention and Executive Influence

Bibby and Davidson (1967) use changes in the composition of the Senate Banking and Currency Committee to explain variation in Senate attention to monetary policy in the late 1950s and early 1960s. Changes in the leadership of the Committee, it is argued, made monetary policy oversight more rewarding for members of Congress. Increased interest in the Senate in the early 1960s is instructive for a few reasons. First, Senate oversight underscores the fact that sustained monetary policy oversight in Congress is rare but not unobservable. Explanations of congressional oversight which completely discount monetary policy choices are unsatisfactory. Second, scrutiny of monetary policy choices in the early 1960s revealed that legislation is not highly important for understanding changes in the Fed. The Vault Cash Act of 1959 and the Federal Reserve Reform Act of 1977 are the most significant amendments to the Federal Reserve Act before 1980, but neither set of rules has a large effect the operating practices of the central bank. Legislation that authorized the purchase of agency issues in 1966 affects operating procedures but is used only sparingly before the appointment of Arthur Burns in 1970. Third, the Senate scrutiny coincides with Fed decisions to coordinate open market activity with Treasury policies that redress the balance of payments problem. As the Fed moved closer to the executive, members of Congress began to more closely monitor Fed choices and practices. This type of congressional response is routine. Woolley and LeLoup (1989) report that congressional oversight activities directed at the Fed are more often than not a function of normative concerns about excessive executive influence over monetary policy outcomes. This finding is consistent with legislators who may exploit central bank intransigence to constrain the executive branch and at the same time create agencies to protect particular economic interests that the central bank may threaten. Central bank autonomy checks executive influence.

Prescriptions for Reform of the Federal Reserve System

The central bank is formally insulated from representative democratic control. There are a mere seven political appointments in the entire System (each for fourteen years) and a statutory exemption from the congressional budget process. These deliberate steps—long terms for members of the Board of Governors and delegation of authority to Reserve Banks—are partly responsible for the inability of presidents to achieve all that they desire from monetary policy. Staff members at the White House under each Administration I studied considered reform of the Fed to increase presidential influence over monetary policy outcomes. Two of the proposals that consistently received the most attention were changes in the term of the Chairman of the Board of Governors of the Federal Reserve System to coincide with the term of the president and presidential appointment of Reserve Bank presidents. Each change would presumably make monetary policy respond to executive preferences. The Fed has supported coincidental terms[2], but objected to appointments of Reserve Bank presidents. Neither proposal received favorable treatment from Congress. Central bank strategy would then appear to benefit members of Congress. Members of Congress certainly have the capacity to update and refine the appointment and budgetary mechanisms of formal political control. But members also have the capacity to create alternative agencies and circumvent central bank institutions to address distributive demands.

Fixed Money Growth Rules and the Distribution of Monetary Restraint

Several unsuccessful reform efforts have attempted to weaken representative control of the money supply. Implicit in efforts to reduce political control is the assumption that central bank discretion inevitably leads to both temptations for and successful use of the money supply to achieve the political ends of elected officials. The problem of control for elected officials centers on how or when the Fed increases the supply of money or restrains the growth of bank credit. The distribution of restraint or exuberance is less important in this context. Prescription for apolitical monetary policy control mechanisms (such as fixed rules for the rate of growth of the money supply) attempt to eliminate the temptation and the practice of political control by specifying strict and public rules for central bank monetary policy choices. These proposals do not address the more complex set of interactions that determines the distribution of the costs and benefits of monetary policy choices.

Friedman (1982) concludes that the members of the Board of Governors of the Fed oppose fixed money growth rate rules and aggregate targets because targets introduce accountability and control. Staff at the Board of Governors of the Federal Reserve System assessed the case for fixed monetary growth rates in 1972. One member of the Board of Governors concluded that the "national priorities as to the allocation of credit" may justify deviation from normative growth targets.[3] Aggregate control mechanisms do not address the underlying distributive struggle that influences monetary policy outcomes. Empirically, distributive incentives and restraints are clearly a part of the political debate over monetary policy. There is no fixed rule for allocation that can resolve or contain conflict over the distribution of scarce credit and capital.

THE DILEMMA OF POLITICAL CONTROL

By using agency rules to vary the costs and benefits of supervision, the central bank can determine the extent to which the preferences of various social actors will be met by indirect central bank action. This source of autonomy has shaped the American political economy in important ways. Some observers laud the independence of the central bank. The breakdown of representative control of the macroeconomy may be salutary and a source of continued stability (Rogoff 1985). For others, the segregation of monetary policy choices from representative control has already undermined American democracy in substantively important ways (Greider 1987). Owners of capital enjoy a privileged source of protection for real returns on investment. This recent publicity of the promise and perils of autonomous central banks has motivated few attempts at reform. There does not seem to be an immediate threat to central bank autonomy that would challenge the existing arrangement. Efforts to reinvigorate representative control have been rare, so the autonomy and impact of the Fed are unlikely to diminish over time. Economic innovations and globally integrated financial markets compel elected officials to delegate more and more authority for outcomes and practices to the central bank and its managers. It would be very surprising if members of the Board of Governors or the Chairman volunteered rules changes or institutional reforms that reduced the autonomy of the Fed. Ultimately, responsibility for control and oversight of monetary policy and the central bank remains the function and choice of members of Congress, but they too seem unlikely to volunteer significant reform.

Continued tolerance of central bank autonomy implies unabated proliferation of federal credit subsidy in periods of monetary restraint and persistently tenuous political control of the macroeconomy. There is some remaining uncertainty about the costs that price stability imposes on the variation and level of real output (Alesina and Gatti, 1995). I would add to the list of potential costs of central bank autonomy the tangible and growing effects of uncoordinated and massive credit subsidies offered by government to privileged borrowers. Overall, the real costs and benefits of central bank autonomy are likely to be to focus of continuing research, but the outcome of the dispute over central bank autonomy is likely to be dominated by considerations about current price levels. If inflation is low, we tolerate and even applaud central bank autonomy. When prices are rising (and nominal interest rates are high), we question and evaluate central bank autonomy. The distributive effects and implications of autonomy rarely inform the controversy.

What should be clear from the postwar experience is that central bankers have an extraordinary role in determining the level and persistence of autonomy. If elected officials chose to challenge central bank autonomy, the ultimate discretion over rules and procedure must nevertheless remain with the central bank. Operating procedures change over time. If social needs for capital diverge from market outcomes, the contemporary rules used to implement monetary policy may be less and less suitable for delivering the types of benefits that elected officials demand from the central bank. The increasingly rapid and global mobility of capital implies that national or regional economic needs will be less and less important as determinants of the flow of capital. Members of Congress interested in affecting the flow of capital using monetary policy are faced with a dilemma. Members of Congress may formally increase representative control and risk executive dominance of central bank choices. Members of Congress may do nothing and tolerate occasional and indirect central bank compliance with political demands. Members of Congress have faced this dilemma in the past: the gains from constraining the executive outweigh the losses associated with the unselective application of monetary restraint. Central bank autonomy will continue to expand as long as members of Congress eschew executive control and Fed decision makers retain discretion over monetary policy institutions. Proponents of central bank autonomy have few reasons to expect change. Critics of central bank autonomy have few options to pursue change given the incentives facing members of Congress.

NOTES

1. Report. c. October, 1977. "Legislation Bearing on the Fed's Independence." Folder: *GAO Audit, June 1976—June 1977.* Box #B51. Papers of Arthur Burns. Gerald R. Ford Library.

2. Memo. Ken Guenther to Arthur Burns. 21 May 1976. Folder: *Coterminous term for Fed Chairman and President* Box #B23. Papers of Arthur Burns. Gerald R. Ford Library.

3. Memo. Partee to Burns. 3 February 1972. Folder: *Wall Street Journal Meeting. 10/02/72.* Box #B114. Papers of Arthur Burns. Gerald R. Ford Library.

References

Aaron, Henry. 1972. *Shelter and Subsidies.* Washington D.C.: The Brookings Institution.

Aberbach, Joel. 1990. *Keeping a Watchful Eye: The Politics of Congressional Oversight*. Washington D.C.: The Brookings Institution.

Ahearn, Daniel S. 1963. *Federal Reserve Policy Reappraised: 1951-59.* New York: Columbia University Press.

Akerlof, George. 1982. "Labor Contracts as a Partial Gift Exchange." *The Quarterly Journal of Economics.* 97:543-69.

Alesina, Alberto and Howard Rosenthal. 1995. *Partisan Politics, Divided Government and the Economy.* New York: Cambridge University Press.

Alesina, Alberto and Jeffrey Sachs. 1988. "Political Parties and the Business Cycle in the United States. 1948-84." *Journal of Money Credit and Banking*. 20:63-82.

Alesina, Alberto and Roberta Gatti. 1995. "Independent Central Bankers: Low Inflation at No Cost?" *American Economic Review.* 85:198-200.

Alesina, Alberto, John Londregan and Howard Rosenthal. 1993. "A Model of the Political Economy of the United States." *The American Political Science Review.* 87:12-33.

Alt, James. 1991. "Leaning into the Wind or Ducking Out of the Storm: U.S. Monetary Policy in the 1980s." In *Macroeconomics and Politics in the 1980s.* Alberto Alesina and Daniel Carliner, eds. Chicago: University of Chicago Press.

Arnold, R. Douglas. 1990. *The Logic of Congressional Action.* New Haven: Yale University Press.

Banaian, King, Leroy Laney, John McArthur and Thomas D. Willett. 1988. "Subordinating the Fed to Political Authorities Will not Control Inflationary Tendencies." In *Political Business Cycles: The Political*

Economy of Money, Inflation, and Unemployment. Thomas Willett, ed. 1988. Durham, N.C.: Duke University Press.

Banks, Jeffrey and Barry Weingast. 1992. "The Political Control of Bureaucracies under Asymmetric Information." *American Journal of Political Science.* 36:509-24.

Baumgartner, Frank and Bryan Jones. 1991. *Agendas and Instability in American Politics.* Chicago: The University of Chicago Press

Beck, Nathaniel. 1984. "Domestic Political Sources of American Monetary Policy: 1955-82." *The Journal of Politics.* 46:786-816.

Beck, Nathaniel. 1987. "Elections and the Fed: is there a political monetary cycle." *American Journal of Political Science.* 31:194-216.

Beck, Nathaniel. 1988. "Politics and Monetary Policy." In *Political Business Cycles: The Political Economy of Money, Inflation, and Unemployment.* Thomas Willett, ed. 1988. Durham, N.C.: Duke University Press.

Beck, Nathaniel. 1990(a). "Testing for a political business cycle with distributed lag models: A note." Presented at the 1990 Annual Meeting of the Political Methodology Society. Washington University, Saint Louis. (July, 1990).

Beck, Nathaniel. 1990(b). "Congress and the Fed: why the dog does not bark in the night." In *The Political Economy of American Monetary Policy.* Thomas Mayer, ed. New York: Cambridge University Press.

Beckhart, Benjamin Haggott. 1972. *Federal Reserve System.* American Institute of Banking. The American Bankers Association. New York: Columbia University Press.

Bendor, Jonathan, Serge Taylor and Roland Van Gaalen. 1985. "Bureaucratic Expertise versus Legislative Authority: A Model of Deception and Monitoring in Budgeting." *American Political Science Review.* 79:1041-60.

Bernanke, Ben and Alan Blinder. 1992. "The Federal Funds Rate and the Channels of Monetary Transmission." *American Economic Review.* 82:901-21.

Bibby, John and Roger Davidson. 1967. *On Capitol Hill: Studies in the Legislative Process.* New York: Holt, Rinehart and Winston, Inc.

Bibby, John. 1968. "Congress' Neglected Function." In Melvin R. Laird, ed. *The Republican Papers.* New York: F.A. Praeger

Birnbaum, Jeffrey and Alan Murray. 1988. *Showdown at Gucci Gulch.* New York: Vintage Books.

Bosworth, Barry, Andrew Carron, and Elisabeth Rhyne. 1987. *The Economics of Federal Credit Programs.* Washington D.C.: The Brookings Institution.

Brennan, Geoffrey and James Buchanan. 1981. "Revenue Implications of Money Creation under Leviathan." *American Economic Review.* 71:347-51.

Buchanan, James and Geoffrey Brennan. 1981. *Monopoly in money and inflation: the case for a constitution to discipline government.* London: Institute of Economic Affairs.

Buckley, Robert, John Tuccillo, and Kevin Villani. 1977. *Capital Markets and the Housing Sector: Perspectives on Financial Reform.* Cambridge, MA: Ballinger Publishing Company.

Calvert, Randall, Mark Moran, and Barry Weingast. 1987. "Congressional influence over policy making: the case of the FTC." In *Congress: Structure and Policy.* Mathew D. McCubbins and Terry Sullivan, eds. New York: Cambridge University Press.

Calvert, Randall, Mathew McCubbins, and Barry Weingast. 1989. "A Theory of Political Control and Agency Discretion." *American Journal of Political Science.* 33:588-611.

Campbell, John and Robert Shiller. 1991. "Yield Spreads and Interest Rate Movements: A Bird's Eye View." *Review of Economic Studies.* 58:495-514.

Cargill, Thomas. 1989. *Central Bank Independence and Regulatory Responsibilities: The Bank of Japan and the Federal Reserve.* New York: Salomon Brothers Center for the Study of Financial Institutions.

Carson, Deane. 1966. "The Bills Only Doctrine in Retrospect." In *Money and Finance: Readings in Theory, Policy, and Institutions.* Deane Carson, ed. New York: John Wiley.

Chandler, Lester. 1970. "Impact of Theory on Policy: The Early Years of the Federal Reserve." In *Men, Money, and Policy: Essays in Honor of Karl R. Bopp.* David Eastburn, ed. Philadelphia: Federal Reserve Bank of Philadelphia.

Chant, John and Keith Acheson. 1972. "The Choice of Monetary Instruments and the Theory of Bureaucracy." *Public Choice.* 12:13-24

Chant, John and Keith Acheson. 1986. "Bureaucratic Theory and the Choice of Central Bank Goals." In *Central Bankers, Bureaucratic Incentives, and Monetary Policy.* Mark Toma and Eugenia Toma, eds. Boston: Kluwer Academic Publishers.

Chappell, Henry, Thomas Harvilesky, and Rob Roy McGregor. 1993. "Partisan Monetary Policies: Presidential Influence Through the Power of Appointment." *The Quarterly Journal of Economics.* 108:185-218.

Cukierman, Alex, Steven B. Webb and Bilin Neyapti. 1994. "Measuring the Independence of Central Banks and Its Effect on Policy Outcomes." *The World Bank Economic Review*. 6:353-98.

Cukierman, Alex. 1992. *Central Bank Strategy, Credibility, and Independence: Theory and Evidence.* Cambridge, MA: The MIT Press.

Degen, Robert. 1987. *The American Monetary System: a concise survey of its evolution since 1896*. Lexington, MA: Lexington Books.

Downs, Anthony. 1967. *Inside Bureaucracy.* Boston: Little, Brown and Co.

Eldredge, Niles and Stephen Jay Gould. 1972. "Punctuated Equilibria: An Alternative to Phyletic Gradualism." In Thomas M. Schopf, ed. *Models in Paleobiology*. San Francisco: Freeman Cooper.

Epstein, Gerald and Juliet Schor. 1989. "The Divorce of the Banca d'Italia and the Italian Treasury: A Case Study of Central Bank Independence." In *State, Market, and Social Regulation: New Perspectives on Italy.* Peter Lange and Marino Regini, eds. New York: Cambridge University Press.

Ferejohn, John and Charles Shipan. 1991. "Congressional Influence on Bureaucracy." *Journal of Law, Economics and Organization.* 6:1-20.

Ferejohn, John. 1986. "Incumbent performance and electoral control." *Public Choice.* 50:5-25.

Fiorina, Morris. 1989. *Congress: Keystone of the Washington Establishment.* New Haven: Yale University Press.

Fisher, Stanley. 1995. "Central Bank Independence Revisited." *American Economic Review.* 85:201-6.

Friedman, Milton. 1962. *Capitalism and Freedom.* Chicago: The University of Chicago Press.

Friedman, Milton. 1982. "Monetary Policy—Theory and Practice." *Journal of Money, Credit and Banking.* 14:98-118

Goff, Brian and Robert Tollison. 1991. "Fed behavior in periods of price and wage controls." *Public Choice.* 70:1-10.

Goldberg, Michael. 1985. "The Relevance of Margin Regulations." *Journal of Money, Credit, and Banking.* 17:521-7.

Goodman, John. 1992. *Monetary Sovereignty: The Politics of Central Banking in Western Europe.* Ithaca: Cornell University Press.

Gouldner, Alvin. 1954. *Patterns of Industrial Bureaucracy.* Glencoe, IL: Free Press.

Grafstein, Robert. 1992. *Institutional Realism: Social and Political Constraints on Rational Actors.* New Haven: Yale University Press.

Greider, William. 1987. *Secrets of The Temple: How the Federal Reserve Runs the Country.* New York: Simon and Schuster.

Grier, Kevin. 1985. *The Political Economy of Monetary Policy: Three Essays.* Ph.D. Department of Economics. Washington University.

Grier, Kevin. 1987. "Presidential elections and Federal Reserve policy: An Empirical Test." *Southern Economic Journal.* 54:475-86.

Grier, Kevin. 1989. "On the Existence of Political Monetary Cycles." *American Journal of Political Science.* 33:376-89

Grier, Kevin. 1991. "Congressional influence on monetary policy: An Empirical Test." *Journal of Monetary Economics.* 28:201-20

Grilli, Vittorio, Donato Masciandaro, and Guido. Tabellini. 1991. "Political and Monetary Institutions and Public Financial Policies in the Industrial Countries. " *Economic Policy.* 6:342-92.

Hargrove, Erwin and Samuel Morley 1987. *The President and the CEA: Interviews with CEA Chairman.* Boulder, CO: Westview Press.

Havrilesky, Thomas. 1987. "A partisanship theory of fiscal and monetary regimes. " *Journal of Money, Credit and Banking.* 19:308-55

Havrilesky, Thomas. 1988. "Two monetary and fiscal policy myths." In *Political Business Cycles: The Political Economy of Money, Inflation, and Unemployment.* Thomas Willett, ed. 1988. Durham, N.C.: Duke University Press.

Havrilesky. Thomas. 1993. *The Pressures on American Monetary Policy.* Boston: Kluwer Academic Publishers

Haynes, Stephen and Joe Stone. 1988. "Does the Political Business Cycle Dominate U.S. Employment and Inflation? Some New Evidence." In *Political Business Cycles: The Political Economy of Money, Inflation, and Unemployment.* Thomas Willett, ed. 1988. Durham, N.C.: Duke University Press.

Hetzel, Robert L. 1990. "The Political Economy of Monetary Policy." In *The Political Economy of American Monetary Policy.* Thomas Mayer, ed. New York: Cambridge University Press.

Hibbs, Douglas. 1987. *The American Political Economy: Macroeconomics and Electoral Politics.* New York: Cambridge University Press.

Hodgman, Donald. 1972. "Selective Credit Controls." *Journal of Money, Credit and Banking.* 4:342-59.

Hunter, William. 1984. "Insurance, incentives and efficiency in small business lending." *Southern Economic Journal.* 50:1171-84.

Ippolito, Dennis. 1984. *Hidden Spending: The Politics of Federal Credit Spending.* Chapel Hill, N.C.: University of North Carolina Press.

Kane, Edward J. 1980. "Politics and Fed Policymaking: The More Things Change the More they Remain the Same." *Journal of Monetary Economics.* 6:199-211.

Kane, Edward J. 1988. "Fedbashing and the Role of Monetary Arrangements in Managing Political Stress." In *Political Business Cycles: The Political Economy of Money, Inflation, and Unemployment.* Thomas Willett, ed. Durham, N.C.: Duke University Press.

Kaufman, Herbert. 1988. "FNMA's Role in Deregulated Markets: Implications from Past Behavior." *Journal of Money, Credit and Banking.* 20:673-83.

Keech, William. 1986. "Elections and Macroeconomic Policy." In *The President and Economic Policy.* James E. Pfiffner, ed. Philadelphia: Institute for the Study of Human Issues.

Kettl, Donald. 1986. *Leadership At the Fed.* New Haven: Yale University Press.

Kidwell, David and Timothy Koch. 1983. "Market Segmentation and the Term Structure of Municipal Yields." *Journal of Money, Credit and Banking.* 15:40-55.

Kiewiet, D. Roderick and Mathew McCubbins. 1991. *The Logic of Delegation: Congressional Parties and the Appropriations Process.* Chicago: The University of Chicago Press.

Klaman, Saul. 1961. *The Postwar Residential Mortgage Market.* Princeton, N.J.: Princeton University Press.

Knight, Jack. 1992. *Institutions and Social Conflict.* New York: Cambridge University Press.

Krasner, Stephen. 1984. "Approaches to the State: Alternative Conceptions and Historical Dynamics." *Comparative Politics.* 16:223-46

Krehbiel, Keith. 1991. *Information and Legislative Organization.* Ann Arbor: The University of Michigan Press.

Kubik, Paul J. 1996. "Federal Reserve Policy During the Great Depression." *Journal of Economic Issues.* 30:829-42.

Kydland, Finn and Edward C. Prescott. 1977. "Rules Rather Than Discretion: The Inconsistency of Optimal Plans." *Journal of Political Economy.* 85:473-92.

Libby, Barbara. 1987. "The Decisionmaking Structure of the Federal Reserve System." *Journal of Economic Issues.* 21:701-12.

Lombra, Raymond. 1988. "Monetary Policy: The Rhetoric versus the Record." In *Political Business Cycles: The Political Economy of Money, Inflation, and Unemployment.* Thomas Willett, ed. 1988. Durham, N.C.: Duke University Press.

Lowi, Theodore. 1964. "American Business, Public Policy, Case Studies, and Political Theory." *World Politics.* 16:677-715

McClure, J. Harold Jr. and Thomas D. Willett. 1988. "The Inflation Tax" In *Political Business Cycles: The Political Economy of Money, Inflation, and Unemployment.* Thomas Willett, ed. 1988. Durham, N.C.: Duke University Press.

McCubbins, Mathew and Thomas Schwartz. 1984. "Congressional Oversight Overlooked: Police Patrols Versus Fire Alarms." *American Journal of Political Science.* 28:165-79.

MacCallum, Bennett. 1995. "Two Fallacies Concerning Central Bank Independence." *American Economic Review.* 85:207-11

Mankiw, Gregory. 1987. "The Optimal Collection of Seignorage: Theory and Evidence." *Journal of Monetary Economics.* 20:327-41.

Mayer, Thomas. 1982. "A Case Study of Federal Reserve Policymaking: Regulation Q in 1966." *Journal of Monetary Economics.* 10:259-71.

Mayer, Thomas. 1990. ed. *The Political Economy of American Monetary Policy.* New York: Cambridge University Press.

Mebane, Walter. 1994. "Fiscal Constraints and Electoral Manipulation in American Social Welfare." *American Political Science Review.* 88:77-94

Meier, Kenneth J. 1985. *Regulation: Politics, Bureaucracy, and Economics.* New York: St. Martin's Press.

Migue, Jean-Luc and Gerard Belanger. 1974. "Towards a General Theory of Managerial Discretion." *Public Choice.* 17:27-47.

Moe, Terry. 1987. "An Assessment of the Positive Theory of Congressional Dominance." *Legislative Studies Quarterly.* 4:475-520

Nathan, Richard. *The Administrative Presidency.* New York: John Wiley.

Newton, Maxwell. 1983. *The Fed: Inside the Federal Reserve, the secret power center that controls the American economy.* New York: Times Books.

Niskanen, William A. 1971. *Bureaucracy and Representative Government.* Chicago, IL: Aldine-Atherton Inc.

Nordhaus, William D. 1975. "The Political Business Cycle." *Review of Economic Studies.* 42:169-90

North, Douglass. 1990. *Institutions, Institutional Change, and Economic Performance.* New York: Cambridge University Press.

Ogul, Morris. 1976. *Congress Oversees the Bureaucracy: Studies in Legislative Supervision.* Pittsburgh: The University of Pittsburgh Press.

O'Hara, Maureen. 1983. "Tax-exempt financing: some lessons from history." *Journal of Money, Credit and Banking.* 15:425-41.

Ostrom, Elinor. 1995. "New Horizons in Institutional Analysis." *American Political Science Review.* 89:174-8

Parker, Glenn. 1992. *Institutional change, discretion, and the making of the modern Congress: an economic interpretation.* Ann Arbor: University of Michigan Press.

Peterson, Peter. 1993. *Facing Up: How to Rescue the Economy from Crushing Debt and Restore the American Dream.* New York: Simon and Schuster.

Phelps, Edmund S. 1973. "Inflation in the Theory of Public Finance." *Swedish Journal of Economics.* 75:68-82.

Pierce, James. 1978. "The Myth of Congressional Supervision of Monetary Policy." *Journal of Monetary Economics.* 4:563-70.

Puckett, Richard. 1984. "Federal Open Market Committee Structure and Decisions. Journal of Monetary Economics." 14:97-104

Rhyne, Elisabeth Holmes. 1988. *Small Business, Banks and SBA Loan Guarantees: Subsidizing the Weak or Bridging a Credit Gap.* New York: Quorum Books.

Ripley, Randall and Grace Franklin. 1991. *Congress, the Bureaucracy, and Public Policy.* 5th edition. Belmont, CA: Wadsworth Publishing Company.

Ritter, Lawrence S. ed. 1980. *Selected Papers of Allan Sproul.* New York: Federal Reserve Bank of New York.

Roberts, Stephen. 1978. "Congressional Oversight of Monetary Policy." *Journal of Monetary Economics.* 4:543-56.

Rogoff, Kenneth. 1985. "The Optimal Degree of Commitment to an Intermediate Monetary Policy Target." *Quarterly Journal of Economics.* 100:1169-89.

Scaggs, Neil T. 1983. "The Federal Reserve System and Congressional Demands for Information. " *Social Science Quarterly.* 64:566-81.

Schaling, Eric. 1995. *Institutions and Monetary Policy: Credibility, Flexibility and Central Bank Independence.* Brookfield, VT: Edward Elgar Publishing.

Schick, Alan, 1980. *Congress and Money: Budgeting, Spending and Taxing.* Washington D.C.: The Urban Institute.

Schick, Alan. 1983. "Politics through Law: Congressional Limitations on Executive Discretion." In Anthony King, ed. *Both Ends of the Avenue: The Presidency, Executive Branch and Congress in the 1980s.* Washington D.C.: American Enterprise Institute for Public Policy Research.

Shay, Robert Paul. 1953. "Regulation W: Experiment in Credit Control." University of Maine Studies, Second Series. University of Maine Bulletin. April, 1953.

Shugart, William and Robert Tollison. 1983. "Preliminary Evidence on the Use of Inputs by the Federal Reserve System." *American Economic Review.* 73:291-304.

Simon, David. 1991. "Segmentation in the Treasury Bill Market: Evidence from Cash Management Bills." *Journal of Financial and Quantitative Analysis.* 26:97-108.

Sims, Christopher. 1980. "Macroeconomics and Reality." *Econometrica.* 48:1-36.

Skowronek, Stephen. 1982. *Building a New Administrative State. The Expansion of National Administrative Capacities: 1877-1920.* New York: Cambridge University Press.

Smith, Vera C. 1990 (1936). *The Rationale of Central Banking.* Indianapolis: Liberty Press.

Spence, David. 1997. "Agency Policy Making and Political Control: Modeling Away the Delegation Problem." *Journal of Public Administration Research and Theory.* 2:199-217.

Spiller, Pablo. 1990. "Agency and the Role of Political Institutions." *Information and Democratic Process.* John A. Ferejohn and James Kuklinski, eds. Chicago: University of Illinois Press.

Spitzer, Robert. 1983. *The Presidency and Public Policy: The Four Arenas of Presidential Power.* University, AL: The University of Alabama Press.

Stein, Herbert. 1994. *Presidential Economics.* 3rd revised edition. Washington D.C: The American Enterprise Institute for Public Policy Research

Thelen, Kathleen and Sven Steinmo. 1992. "Historical Institutionalism in Comparative Perspective." In *Structuring Politics: Historical Institutionalism in Comparative Perspective.* Sven Steinmo, Kathleen Thelen, and Frank Longstreth, eds. New York: Cambridge University Press.

Timberlake, Richard Henry. 1965. *Money, Banking and Central Banking.* New York: Harper and Row.

Toma, Mark and Eugenia F. Toma. 1986. *Central Banks, Bureaucratic Incentives, and Monetary Policy.* Boston: Kluwer Academic Publishers.

Toma, Mark. 1982. "Inflationary Bias of the Federal Reserve System: A Bureaucratic Perspective." *Journal of Monetary Economics.* 10:163-90.

Tufte, Edwin R. 1978. *Political Control of the Economy.* Princeton: Princeton University Press.

Weintraub, Robert. 1978. "Congressional Supervision of Monetary Policy." *Journal of Monetary Economics.* 4:341-62.

Wells, Wyatt. 1994. *Economist in an Uncertain World: Arthur F. Burns and the Federal Reserve, 1970-78.* New York: Columbia University Press.

Wheelock, David C. 1991. *The Strategy and Consistency of Federal Reserve monetary policy, 1924-33.* New York: Cambridge University Press.

White, Lawrence. 1988. "Problems Inherent in Political Money Supply Regimes: Some Historical and Theoretical Lessons." In *Political Business Cycles: The Political Economy of Money, Inflation, and Unemployment.* Thomas Willett, ed. 1988. Durham, N.C.: Duke University Press.

Willett, Thomas. ed. 1988. *Political Business Cycles: The Political Economy of Money, Inflation, and Unemployment.* Durham, NC: Duke University Press.

Wilson, James Q. 1988. *Bureaucracy: What Government Agencies Do and Why They Do It.* New York: Basic Books.

Wilson, James Q. ed. 1980. *The Politics of Regulation.* New York: Basic Books.

Wood, B. Dan and Richard Waterman. 1994. *Bureaucratic Dynamics: The Role of Bureaucracy in a Democracy.* Boulder, CO: Westview Press.

Woolley, John and Lance LeLoup. 1989. "The Adequacy of the Electoral Motive in Explaining Legislative Attention to Monetary Policy." *Comparative Politics.* 22:63-82

Woolley, John. 1984. *Monetary Politics: The Federal Reserve and the Politics of Monetary Policy.* New York: Cambridge University Press.

Woolley, John. 1985. "Central banks and inflation." In *The Politics of Inflation and Stagnation: Theoretical Approaches and Individual Case Studies.* Leon Lindberg and Charles Maier, eds. Washington D.C.: The Brookings Institution.

Woolley, John. 1988. "Partisan Manipulation of the Economy: Another Look at Monetary Policy with Moving Regression." *Journal of Politics.* 50:335-60.

Worsham, Jeff, Marc Eisner and Evan Ringquist. 1997. "Assessing the Assumptions: A Critical Analysis of Agency Theory." *Administration and Society*. 28:419-40.

Index